FROM
ROMANOV
TO
GORBACHEV

Russia in the 20th Century

PETER MANTIN

COLIN LANKESTER

Hutchinson

London   Sydney   Auckland   Johannesburg

Hutchinson Education

An imprint of Century Hutchinson Ltd

62–65 Chandos Place, London WC2N 4NW

Century Hutchinson Australia (Pty) Ltd
89–91 Albion Street, Surry Hills, NSW 2010

Century Hutchinson New Zealand Limited
PO Box 40–086, Glenfield, Auckland 10

Century Hutchinson South Africa (Pty) Ltd
PO Box 337, Bergvlei 2012, South Africa

First published 1989

Set in Times and Helvetica

Designed by Heather Richards

Printed and bound in Great Britain by
Scotprint Ltd., Musselburgh

British Library Cataloguing in Publication Data
Mantin, Peter
    From Romanov to Gorbachev: Russia in the 20th century. –
    (Hutchinson history series).
    1. Soviet Union 1894
    I. Title   II. Lankester, Colin
    947.08′3
    ISBN 0-09-182378-1

To Julie, Ben and Hannah

Contents

Background to Revolution   4
Tsar Nicholas   6
The countryside in 1900   8
The towns in 1900   10
Sources Test: 'Bloody Sunday' 1905   12
Opposition to the Tsar   14
Revolutionary Groups   16
The Revolutionaries: Lenin, Trotsky and Stalin   18
World War I and Revolution   21
Coursework Exercise: The Russian Revolution   24
The Provisional Government   25 *read.*
Lenin in Power   28
The Civil War 1918–21   31
Lenin's last days 1923–24   34
The Struggle for Power   36
Collectivisation: theory   37
Collectivisation: practice   40
Coursework Exercise: Stalin and Industrialisation   42
The Purges   46
The policy of the Purges   48
Sources Test: Cult of personality   50
Soviet foreign policy   53
Operation Barbarossa   55
Stalingrad   57
Looking at Eastern Europe   59
Yalta   60
Coursework Exercise: Soviet War Propaganda   62
Cold War   64
The Marshall Plan   66
Stalin's Last Years 1945–53   68
Stalin: man or monster?   70
NATO   71
The Warsaw Pact   72
The Thaw 1953–61   73
Hungarian and Czech crises   75
Khrushchev, 1953–64   78
The Brezhnev Years   80
The Arms Race   82
Glasnost and Perestroika   84
Up to date   86

Revision Section
Men who ruled Russia   88
Romanov to Lenin   89
Lenin to Stalin   90
Events inside Russia   91
Stalin to Gorbachev   92
Russia and the World   93

Glossary   94
Index   95

Background to Revolution

Russia was the first country in the world to have a successful communist revolution. It took place in 1917.

If we are to understand how and why this happened we will need to know more about the country and its people.

Look at the evidence on these two pages and try to work out how difficult Russia was to rule.

The Russian Empire in 1900 contained a large number of different people (see Source **A**.) Another way in which these people could be divided up can be seen in Source **D**.

A Population of the different races in the Russian Empire, 1897 in round figures.

Great Russians	55,650,000
Ukrainians	22,400,000
White Russians	5,900,000
Poles	7,900,000
Lithuanians	1,650,000
Letts	1,400,000
Estonians	1,000,000
Finns	2,500,000
Germans	1,800,000
Romanians	1,100,000
Jews	5,000,000
Georgians	1,350,000
Armenians	1,150,000
Caucasian mountaineers	1,000,000
Iranians	1,000,000
Tartars	3,700,000
Kirghiz	4,000,000
Other Asiatic people	5,750,000
Mongols	500,000
Others	200,000

B Political map of the Russian Empire, 1900

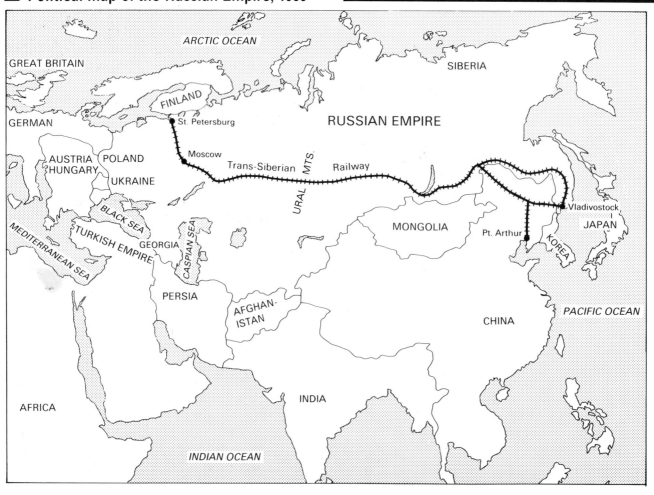

In 1900 Russia was ruled by Tsar Nicholas II. Nicholas was the Tsar of the Russian Empire. The Tsar had complete power over the country. He ruled Russia as an autocrat. This meant that he ruled on his own without a Duma (parliament). He relied on the nobles for help and support. The peasants and workers were not asked for their advice. They did not have the vote.

Nicholas had ministers chosen from the nobles to help him rule, but he could sack them at any time, and often did. Any opposition to the government was dealt with harshly by the secret police, the Okhrana. Nicholas also used the army to crush those who opposed him. The Russian Orthodox Church supported the Tsar and taught the people to respect him. The Church was rich and owned a lot of land.

C **The Tsar of All the Russias with his wife, the Tsarina.**

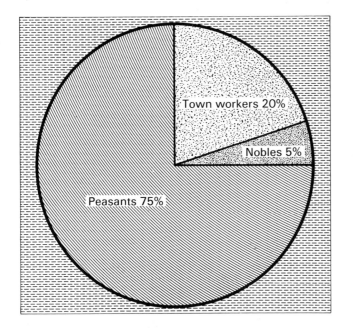

D **Chart showing the different social classes in the Russian Empire, 1900.**

Questions

1 Look at Source **B**.
  a Make a list of countries which border the Russian empire.
  b How does the size of Russia compare with that of other countries on the map?
  c Can you see from Source **B** how Russia was trying to solve the problem of its size?
  d In what ways are maps like Source **B** valuable as evidence to a historian of the Russian Revolution?

2 Explain the meaning of the following words: revolution, empire, Tsar, autocrat, Duma, Okhrana.

3 Source **A** is taken from the Census of 1897.
  a What is a census?
  b What evidence is there in Source **A** to suggest that these are not accurate figures?
  c Why would it be difficult to take an accurate census in the Russia of 1900?

4 Looking back at all the sources in this chapter what clues can you find to suggest that Russia was a difficult country to govern?

Tsar Nicholas

A **Tsar Nicholas II and his wife Alexandra.** A photograph taken in 1913, to celebrate 300 years of the rule of Nicholas's family, the Romanovs.

We can gain a good idea of the way Nicholas was seen by his people by looking at photographs of him.

Other sources provide clues as to how Nicholas saw his responsibilities.

When looking at these sources try and work out how fit he was to govern an empire like Russia.

B **An extract from the diary of Tsar Nicholas II, October 1894** (on the day he became Tsar).

"

What is going to happen to me, to all Russia? I am not prepared to be the Tsar. I never wanted to become one. I know nothing of the business of ruling. I have no idea of even how to talk to ministers.

"

C **From 'Papa Tsar' a biography of Tsar Nicholas II**

"

Nicholas disliked making decisions and above all he disliked saying disagreeable things to people . . . Frequently a minister left the palace after a pleasant talk with the Tsar to find a letter of dismissal awaiting him when he arrived home . . . The Tsar was weak and he was also very shy. He disliked public life and public duties . . . Nicholas made no attempt to see for himself what went on in his Empire. He never visited factories, schools or industrial areas in the towns.

"

D **Statement by Leon Trotsky, 1932**

"

His ancestors did not bequeath him one quality which would have made him capable of governing an empire.

"

E **Comment on Nicholas II by an anonymous Russian Cabinet Minister.**

"

Nicholas II was not fit to run a village post office.

"

Nicholas was a family man. He would rather be with his children than go to meetings with his government. He was very worried about his son Alexis, who had a disease called haemophilia. This meant that his blood would not clot, so he would bleed to death if he cut himself.

Nicholas was heavily influenced by his wife. She did not want him to be a constitutional monarch. This means that she did not want him to share power with an elected group of people, like a Duma or Parliament.

F Tsar Nicholas II blessing his troops during World War I. He is holding in his hand a sacred icon (holy picture).

The Tsar's wife wrote letters to her husband whilst he was away commanding the armies at the front in World War I. These tell us how the Government was run.

G Letter from the Tsar's wife Alexandra to Tsar Nicholas, about 1915.

"

Never forget you ARE and MUST remain autocratic Emperor; we are not yet ready for a constitutional government . . .

. . . we have been placed by God on a throne and we must keep it firm and give it over to our son untouched – if you keep that in mind you will remember to be the sovereign and how much easier for an autocratic sovereign than one who has sworn to the Constitution.

"

Questions

1 a Describe Nicholas's clothes in the photographs (**A** and **F**).
  b These photographs were taken for a reason. What impression do you think the Tsar wanted his people to have of him? List what you can see in the photographs to support your answer.
2 Make a list of the evidence on these pages which shows Nicholas as being
  a a good ruler.
  b a bad ruler.
  Which list is the longer?
3 a Read Source **E**. How does the impression of Nicholas in this source differ from that given in the photographs?
  b Why do you think these sources give such different impressions of the same person?
4 Historical sources are useful for different reasons. What is the value to the historian of Nicholas II of using diaries (as in Source **B**) as a source of evidence?
5 Look again at the sources and your answers to the questions. How suited do you think Nicholas was to the job of governing Russia? Give reasons for your answer.

The countryside in 1900

The following information gives evidence about how most of the Russian people lived in 1900. As you look at the evidence try to work out how serious a problem this was for the Tsar.

Questions

1 What evidence is there in Source **A** to suggest that the people were
   a poor?
   b unhealthy?
2 **a** Who might have taken photograph **A** and why?
   b Was this photograph posed? Explain your answer with reference to things in the photograph.
   c The same source can provide evidence for different historians. How could photograph **A** be useful for:
      i historians of fashion?
      ii historians of buildings?
      iii historians of photography?
3 Photograph **C** was 'posed'. Does that mean that it is of no value to the historian of life in Russia in 1900?
4 Which of these two photographs more accurately shows the living conditions of most of the Russian people in 1900? Explain your answer.

B **Description of a traveller's visit to the Russian countryside in about 1900.**

“

By Western standards Russian agriculture was backward. The peasants farmed with simple hand tools, used wooden ploughs, and had but a few animals to speed up the process. Most peasants had been serfs until 1861. They had worked on their master's land as his private possessions, with no rights to move away or even to marry without his permission. They could be bought or sold and were, on occasion, even gambled away at the card table. Tsar Alexander II had freed serfs in 1861, yet their lot had not greatly improved. The village community had been given land, but it had to be paid for over 49 years. This, together with the pressure of an increasing population on the land available, meant that great hardship continued for the majority. Their day-to-day concern with mere survival contrasted sharply with the wealth, education, and lifestyle of the tiny minority of rich landowners and nobles, and with the royal household in the capital.

”

C The Tsarina and her four daughters.

E Extracts from 'The Empire of the Tsar' by Tony Howarth, a school book about Russia (Longmans, 1980).

"

As the population grew, the land was redistributed into smaller and smaller parcels. . . .

The peasants suffered high rates of taxation on their land and on goods they bought from the towns. . . .

The average crop yields in Russia were similar to those in England in the Middle Ages. . . .

Many poorer peasants had to work for landlords in order to earn enough to pay their taxes. In good times when few starved, the peasants looked at the great estates in envy. In bad times when harvests were poor, envy could turn to blind hatred as peasants looted and burned landlords' property.

"

D **Death in infancy** (the number of children who died before the age of one out of every 1000 born alive) **in different countries in 1900.**

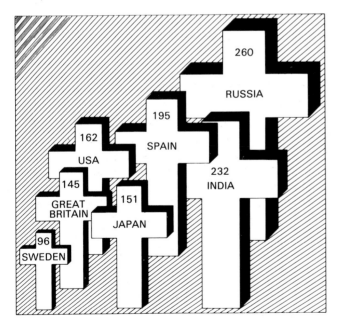

260 RUSSIA

195 SPAIN

162 USA

232 INDIA

145 GREAT BRITAIN

151 JAPAN

96 SWEDEN

Questions

5 How do the other sources help explain Russia's position in the 'Death in Infancy Table' in Source **D**?

Include quotations from more than one source in your answer.

6 You are the inheritor of a large estate in Russia in 1905. You are visiting a village on your estate for the first time, having been brought up in the capital, St Petersburg. You might be shocked!

Look at the photograph in Source **A**. What improvements might you want to make to the village? Remember to be realistic, bearing in mind that improvements cost money and *you* have to pay.

The towns in 1900

In the previous chapter you made a judgement about how serious you thought the problem of the peasants' living conditions were.

As you read the evidence here, try and work out whether conditions of the town workers were any better than those of the people in the countryside.

In 1900 Russia was experiencing important changes. Look at these figures.

A Changes in industrial production in Russia, 1890–1900.

	1890	1900
Coal (in millions of tonnes)	6	16.2
Oil (in million of tonnes)	4.6	10.7
Pig Iron (in millions of tonnes)	0.9	2.9
Steel (in millions of tonnes)	0.8	2.2
Railways (in thousands of kilometres)	30.6	53.2

B Comparison of the Russian economy in 1900 with the leading European industrial countries.

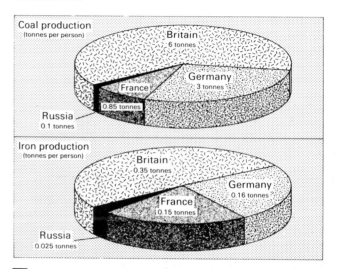

Coal production (tonnes per person)
Britain 6 tonnes
Germany 3 tonnes
France 0.85 tonnes
Russia 0.1 tonnes

Iron production (tonnes per person)
Britain 0.35 tonnes
Germany 0.16 tonnes
France 0.15 tonnes
Russia 0.025 tonnes

C A lodging house in Moscow around 1900
(People who could not afford the cost of a bed had to sleep on the floor under the beds.)

So, although Russian industry was developing, it was still well behind the countries of Western Europe.

D Street scene in St. Petersburg, 1900.

E Description by a factory inspector of a barracks built for male workers in a metal working factory in a Russian town around 1900.

"
These dwellings can be compared without any exaggeration with the quarters of animals: their unwashed and filthy condition are unfit for humans. Even in summer, when the windows and doors are open, the air in them is stifling; on the walls and the bunks are traces of slime and mould, and the floors are barely visible for the filth which sticks to them.
"

F Statement by doctors and medical workers at a conference in St Petersburg, 1900.

"
The sound and proper fight against infant mortality, alcoholism, tuberculosis, syphilis, and other common diseases, representing in Russia social ills of great importance, is possible only under conditions guaranteeing the broad spread of information about their causes and prevention, and for this, full freedom of person, speech, press and assembly are necessary.
"

G An American report on Russian cities in 1900.

"
The first thing that strikes your attention is a curious detail. All the shops that offer wares to the people do so, not in words, as with us, but with pictures. Why is this? Simply because the majority of their customers cannot read!
"

Questions

1 Look at Source **A**. Was there a big increase in industrial production in Russia between 1890 and 1900? Quote figures from this source to back up your answer. yes

2 Look at photograph **C**.
   a What did the workers use for tables and how did each family divide up its living space in the room?
   b Does photograph **C** prove that all town workers in Russia in 1900 had very bad living conditions? Explain your answer.

3 Compare photograph **C** with photograph **A** in the previous chapter.
   How similar were conditions for peasants and town workers? Explain your answer.

4 All sources of evidence can be biased. Some are biased in different ways. What difference do you notice in the bias in Sources **E** and **F**? Why do you think there is a difference?

5 Having looked at sources **A** to **G**, do you think the living conditions of the town workers were likely to be a problem for the Tsar? Explain your answer.

6 Compare the evidence about conditions in the towns with those in the countryside. Were conditions in the towns any better than those for people living in rural areas? Give reasons for your answer.

'Bloody Sunday' 1905

The Tsar was facing increasing pressure to improve the living conditions of the peasants and workers. A series of bad harvests led to peasant uprisings and workers' strikes. The Japanese attack on the Russian naval base at Port Arthur on the Pacific coast in 1904 (see Source **B** page 4) made things worse. The Tsar had to pay for the war from taxes. It was the workers and peasants who paid the taxes.

Unfortunately the Tsar underestimated the rising power of the Japanese, and the Russian navy was defeated at the battle of Tsushima in 1905. The war was lost. This brought about more protest and criticism. On January 22nd, 1905 a group of workers led by a priest called Father Gapon marched towards the Tsar's Palace in St Petersburg. They were carrying a petition signed by 135,000 people. That petition tells us about some of their complaints.

A Petition to the Tsar, composed by Father Gapon and carried by him at the head of the procession on Sunday, 22nd January 1905.

"

We ask but little; to reduce the working day to provide a minimum wage of a rouble a day and to abolish overtime. Officials have brought the country to complete ruin and involved it in a shameful war. We working men have no voice in the way the enormous amounts raised from us in taxes are spent.

"

B Painting of 'Bloody Sunday', 22nd January 1905.

The Tsar's troops were waiting for Father Gapon and the demonstrators. Suddenly the Cossack troops attacked them and cut their way with swords through to the back of the crowd. Then the troops opened fire. (see Source **B**).

Official figures show that 96 people were killed and 333 wounded. However, as many of the injured were taken home for treatment the real figure was probably much higher. The Tsar had spent that day at his palace at Tsarskoe Selo. He heard of the trouble and wrote these words in his diary.

C Extract from the diary of Tsar Nicholas II, 22nd January 1905.

"

22nd January, Sunday. A painful day! There have been serious disorders in St Petersburg because workmen wanted to come up to the Winter Palace. Troops had to open fire in several places in the city. There were many killed and wounded. God, how painful and sad! Mama arrived from town, straight to Mass. I lunched with all the others. Went for a walk with Misha. Mama stayed overnight.

"

However, other people saw this event quite differently. These are the words of Leon Trotsky, who became one of the leaders of the Russian Revolution in 1917.

D Description of 'Bloody Sunday' by the revolutionary, Leon Trotsky.

"

'Let us through to the Tsar!' The old ones fell on their knees. The women begged and the children begged. 'Let us through to the Tsar!' – and then it happened! The guns went off with thunder . . . The snow reddened with workers' blood . . . Tell all and sundry in what way the Tsar has dealt with the toilers of St Petersburg . . .

"

E Photograph of 'Bloody Sunday', 22 January 1905.

Questions

1 How did the soldiers stop the Bloody Sunday demonstration? (Say which sources you got your information from.)
2 Read Source **A**. In what ways can this petition be useful to the historian of Bloody Sunday?
3 Read Sources **C** and **D**.
   a What differences do you notice between the two descriptions of 'Bloody Sunday'?
   b Why do you think the descriptions are so different?
4 Look at all these sources.
   "The events of Bloody Sunday prove that the Tsar's policy was to crush workers' protests in a violent way."
   Do the sources show this view to be true? Explain your answer fully.
5 Source **B** is a painting; Source **E** is a photograph. 'A photograph must be a more reliable source than a painting.' Do you agree?

Opposition to the Tsar

The previous chapters have shown that there were several basic problems facing Tsar Nicholas II at the beginning of this century. It may not suprise you to learn that there was a lot of opposition to the Tsar. In the end, in 1917, Nicholas was forced to give up his throne in a revolution.

Whilst you are looking at the evidence about the opposition to the Tsar, think about these questions. Remember that the work you have already done should help you:

a Why were people opposed to the Tsar?

b What did the Tsar do about the opposition?

c Were the Tsar's actions likely to cause trouble later on?

d Was a violent revolution the only solution to the problem?

e What chances were there of a violent revolution succeeding?

The events of Bloody Sunday helped bring about strikes in many towns in Russia. Although Nicholas had not given the order to open fire on the workers, he was blamed by many people for Bloody Sunday because he was the autocrat (that is the sole ruler of a country who does not want to share power).

Foreigners who were staying in St Petersburg at the time give us an idea of the way in which the people now saw the Tsar.

A A cartoon entitled 'Peace and Quiet' which appeared in 1906 in Flag, one of the many underground journals that were distributed in the cities of Russia at this time.

'Peace and Quiet'. 'Znamya' (Flag) No.1. 1906.

B Statement by the U.S. Consul in St Petersburg, January 1905.

"

After Bloody Sunday the Russian people will never trust or love the Tsar again.

"

Revolutionary Councils of workers and soldiers called 'Soviets' were set up. There were strikes and outbreaks of violence in the streets. Other revolutionaries like Trotsky returned to Russia to try and help overthrow the government. There were riots in other parts of the country. Nicholas used troops and the secret police to arrest the leaders of the Soviets and to stop the riots in the streets. Some of the leaders of the Revolution were put in jail. Others escaped abroad.

However, Nicholas did agree to some changes which he outlined in the 'October Manifesto', including the setting up of a new Duma (parliament). This was a great chance for him to bring about real changes in the way in which Russia was governed.

The Duma was controlled by nobles and middle classes, but it put forward demands which the Tsar would not meet. It demanded more say in the running of the country than the Tsar was prepared to allow. Once Nicholas had restored law and order he made it clear that he had no intention of giving up his power. He declared that 'the Emperor of All Russia has supreme autocratic power. It is given by God' and it was everybody's duty to obey the Tsar. The first Duma was soon closed down, as was the second one, in May 1907. The government then changed the qualification for the vote so that landlords had much more power than the peasants. As a result, the third Duma rarely caused the Tsar any problems, and lasted its full five years until 1912, as did the fourth Duma to 1917. The Tsar took little notice of the majority of his people.

Questions

1 **Look at the cartoon in Source A.**
   a Who or what do you think is represented by the figure of the skeleton on horseback?
   b What do you think the title of the cartoon is trying to say?
   c What do you think was the attitude of the person who drew this cartoon to the events in Russia at this time?
2 Hundreds of illegal journals like Flag were published in Russia at this time with cartoons like Sources **A** and **C** in them.
   What sort of effect do you think they would have had on the people who saw them?
3 a In what way did the government ensure that the third Duma gave the Tsar few problems?
   b Why do you think this would have been a less 'troublesome' Duma?

Follow-on question

4 In the chapter on Tsar Nicholas we saw that, in many ways, the Tsar was a weak ruler. However, on 'Bloody Sunday' he seems to have acted with strength. Was he behaving differently or in the same way he had behaved before? Explain your answer.

C Back cover of journal: "In this world there is a tsar. He is without pity. HUNGER is his name."

Revolutionary Groups

During Tsar Nicholas's reign several groups had been formed with the aim of changing the way in which Russia was governed. They were called 'revolutionaries'. A revolution is a rapid change and they were planning a sudden change in the government of Russia. The ideas of some of these groups are described in Source **B**.

Many of the people who joined these groups were educated people who believed that they could improve the conditions of the people only by overthrowing the Tsar. They split into many groups, each of which had its own ideas about the best way of 'saving' Russia.

Many of these groups were influenced by the ideas of Karl Marx (1818–1883). He was a German writer who was forced to leave his own country and settled in London. His ideas appear in books like 'Das Kapital' and the 'Communist Manifesto'. They include the beliefs that:

B The ideas of Karl Marx.

"

All of history can be seen as a struggle for power between classes, the 'Haves' and the 'Have-nots'.

▼

The final struggle will be between the Capitalists (middle class factory and landowners) and the Proletariat (people who work for the capitalists for low wages and in bad conditions).

▼

The Capitalists will not give up power without a fight, so a violent revolution will be needed.

▼

These revolutions will first take place in the industrial countries of western Europe, where there are most Proletariat.

▼

After the revolution a Socialist government will rule the country and take over the banks, land and factories on behalf of the people.

▼

Once all the Capitalists have been removed there will be no need for a government. The people will live together on equal terms in a state of Communism.

"

C Political cartoon drawn about 1900.
The Russians words on the cartoon say, top tier: 'We rule over you'; second tier: 'We govern you'; third tier: We fool you'; fourth tier: 'We shoot you'; fifth tier; 'We eat instead of you'; bottom tier: 'We work for you; we feed you.'
The lines below it say:
'The time will come – The people will rise up in revolt;
They will straighten their bent back,
And with a concerted, mighty heave of the shoulders
They will topple this edifice.'

From 1906–1911 Peter Stolypin was Prime Minister. He introduced a series of changes. He encouraged peasants to buy their own land and tried to improve working conditions in the towns. He aimed to stop the revolutionaries. Stolypin was assassinated in 1911 and there were rumours that the Tsar was linked with his death. Stolypin had fallen out of favour with the Tsar when he criticised the Tsar's favourite, Rasputin (see page 23). There were several industrial strikes between 1912 and 1914. The strikers wanted more reforms, but the Tsar's government would not allow them. Revolutionary activity increased after 1912.

This suggests that the Tsar was not prepared to give up any of his power or tackle the basic problems in his Empire.

C Some of the ideas of revolutionary groups.

The Social Revolutionary Party, 1901

- Wanted a peasants' revolution.
- Wanted to get rid of the Tsar using violent methods.
- Killed the Tsar's uncle in 1905 and murdered other members of the government.

Questions

1 Look at Source A.
   a Who is supposed to be shown on each level of the cartoon?
   b Why do you think they are shown like this?
   c Who do you think might have drawn this cartoon? Explain your answer.
   d The cartoon is biased. In what way?
   e If the cartoon is biased, does that mean it is unreliable? Give reasons for your answer.
2 Look back at this chapter and at the chapter on Bloody Sunday. Write an article for a revolutionary newspaper, explaining why the workers of St Petersburg decided to petition the Tsar in 1905. Use examples of their living and working conditions in your article.
3 Look back at the questions raised on page 14. Use the information and sources to help you answer as many of the questions as you can.
4 Looking back at the 1905 Revolution, the Tsar had a good chance to change things for the better. Why do you think he did not do so?

The Social Democratic Party, 1898. Split into two groups in 1903.

Bolsheviks

- Wanted to get rid of the Tsar.
- Wanted Workers' Revolution but without middle class help.
- Led by a small group of educated people.
- Many of the leaders went abroad.
- Would use violence if necessary.

Mensheviks

- Wanted to get rid of the Tsar in a Workers' Revolution with middle class help.
- Led by middle class educated people.
- Not keen on using violence.

The Revolutionaries

Lenin (1870–1924)

Vladimir Ilyich Ulyanov (later known as Lenin) was the son of an Inspector of Schools and his family was quite well off. He was a very clever, hard working student, who read widely and discussed politics with his family. His elder brother, Alexander, was involved in revolutionary activities, and was executed for trying to assassinate Tsar Alexander III.

Vladimir won a place at Kazan University to study law. He was a brilliant scholar, but was expelled for refusing to give up his revolutionary activities. He wrote many books and pamphlets calling on the workers and peasants to rise up and overthrow the Tsar. The revolution would follow the ideas of Karl Marx and would eventually lead to Communism (see page 16). Like many revolutionaries, he took false names to hide from the secret police, but his writings were thought to be so revolutionary that when he was caught he was sent to Siberia. This did not stop him from smuggling revolutionary articles out of Russia.

In 1900 he left Russia with his wife, Nadezhda Krupskaya, who was also a revolutionary and supported him in the long years abroad in exile. Lenin lived in London for a time. He organised a revolutionary paper called 'Iskra' (The Spark), publishing articles from revolutionaries all over Europe and indeed smuggled out of Russia. 'Iskra' was itself then smuggled back into Russia.

One of the writers was Trotsky. When they met in London and on a walk gazed at the Houses of Parliament, Lenin said, 'This is *their* Parliament,' meaning not just the British but all enemies of the Communists.

In 1903 the Conference of the Communist Party was held in London. One group of Communists wanted to gain the support of the middle classes rather than the peasants. Another group, led by Lenin, wanted a small, well organised Party of revolutionaries to gain the support of peasants and workers for the Communist Revolution. Lenin's side won the day and became known as the 'Bolsheviks' (majority). The others were the 'Mensheviks' (minority). (See Revolutionary Groups, Source **C**, page 17).

Lenin was not in Russia when the Revolution of 1905 broke out, and when it failed he was depressed. It seemed that the Revolution might never come true.

A **Letter from Lenin in 1907 to a young Bolshevik from Georgia** (who had tried to raise funds for the Communist Party by running brothels).

> "
> I am not concerned with whether you have affairs with women or not, and I am also not concerned with whether you change them as often as you change your shirts. But I am concerned with the good name of our Bolshevik Party. I cannot agree that it is the right policy for our Party to be concerned with the brothels which you have organised.
> "

The letter was sent to a man who called himself Stalin.

When the first Revolution of 1917 broke out, Lenin was in Switzerland. Events had again taken place in Russia without the leader of the Bolsheviks. He desperately wanted to get to Russia, but Germany controlled most of the land between. Even though the German leaders hated Communism, they let Lenin's train go through to Petrograd with Lenin concealed within. The long wait seemed to be over.

B Lenin, 1893

Leon Trotsky (1879–1940)

The man who became known as Trotsky and was to go down in history as one of the leaders of the Bolshevik Revolution was born Lev Davidovitch Bronstein. He was the son of a Jewish farmer in the Russian province of Kherson. Only much later, to escape the attentions of the secret police, did he take the name of Trotsky from a former jailer.

His father was a kulak (a rich peasant) who owned 700 acres of land and employed many peasants. Trotsky was encouraged to read at home and was top of his class at school. He started a school magazine and wrote most of it himself. He joined in discussion groups with other young people who opposed the Tsar.

Trotsky began to write pamphlets and articles criticising the Tsar's government and encouraging workers to go on strike. For this activity he was sent into political exile in the frozen wastes of the Arctic Circle in Siberia.

A Trotsky's photograph from the Tsar's secret police files.

Trotsky used his time in exile to read books by Karl Marx and Lenin. He also wrote articles for Lenin's revolutionary newspaper 'Iskra'. These articles were so good that he became known as 'The Pen'.

He decided to escape, leaving behind his wife and two babies, and join other leading revolutionaries in western Europe. In 1902 Trotsky and Lenin met for the first time in London. They did not always agree and, indeed, Trotsky first joined Lenin's revolutionary opponents, the Mensheviks. It was not until 1917 that he joined the Bolsheviks, so it is not surprising that some Bolsheviks were suspicious of him.

In 1905 Trotsky returned to Russia to take part in the Revolution of 1905 which followed the 'Bloody Sunday' demonstration.

With the failure of this revolution, Trotsky again left Russia, eventually becoming a journalist in America. When the Tsar's government began to collapse in early 1917, Trotsky returned to Petrograd a month after Lenin and was greeted as a hero at the Finland Station. He now fully supported Lenin and used his organisational talent to plan the Bolshevik takeover of power (see page 26).

B Trotsky's part in these days has been described by an eyewitness, N. Sukhanov:

> ... it seemed that he spoke everywhere simultaneously. Every worker and soldier of Petrograd knew him and listened to him. His influence on the masses and leaders alike was overwhelming. He was the central figure of those days, and the chief hero of this remarkable chapter of history.

Stalin (1879–1953)

Joseph Djugashvili was born in a small house in the province of Georgia in the south of the Russian Empire. His father worked in a local boot factory and used to beat his wife when he was drunk. Indeed he was killed in a drunken brawl when Joseph was only 11. Joseph hated his father but loved his mother, a hard-working washerwoman who saved to send her son to priest's training college. He was a conscientious student who had to overcome many difficulties. A terrible attack of smallpox had left him scarred for life; his arm was smashed so badly in an accident that it remained shorter than the other.

Soon Stalin began to read forbidden books, take a great interest in politics and sneak out of college to take part in meetings with workers and students. He was expelled in 1899, became a Bolshevik, and was imprisoned by the secret police.

A Stalin from the secret police files.

Stalin changed his name at least 23 times so as to escape the secret police. He came to the attention of Lenin through his daring attempts to get money for the Bolshevik party, including robbing banks. He read Lenin's paper 'Iskra' and organised workers' strikes in Georgia. Despite these activities he was not well known to most party members. He did not take part in the Revolution of 1905 and spent much time in exile in Siberia. He began to be nicknamed 'Stalin', which means 'man of steel'.

Stalin's wife died of tuberculosis in 1907. He became a member of the Bolshevik Central Committee in 1912 and edited the official party newspaper 'Pravda' (which means 'truth'.) Soon he was imprisoned for the sixth time. He was only released from Siberia after the Tsar's abdication in 1917 and made his way to Petrograd. For all his activity, Stalin was not one of the heroes of the Revolution.

B An account of Stalin by a prison officer who guarded him.

"

Whenever he could, he read – and the books were not those that the Government approved of. Once I remember, I had to order him to be flogged – for he had been preaching rebellion to the prisoners. He turned up for punishment, reading one of his books. The blows fell. He continued to read. The senior warder ordered him to lay down his book, but he merely went on reading. The book was torn from his hand and thrown to the floor and he was whipped again. He did not cry out, though the punishment was savage. And when it was all over and his hands were freed, he picked up his book and carried on reading it as if what had happened had just been a trivial interruption.

"

C Comment by person who took a part in the Revolution.

"

All I remember of Stalin is that he seemed like a grey blur – somebody you would hardly notice against the landscape.

"

Questions

1 What were these leaders of the Russian Revolution like? What clues in their stories show the sort of people they were?
2 Compare the story of Lenin with the stories of Trotsky and Stalin. Do you think Lenin's story was more like that of Stalin or of Trotsky? Give examples to explain your answer.
3 Why do you think the Germans decided to allow Lenin's train through to Russia in March 1917?
4 Do you believe the account of Stalin in prison? Explain your answer using the source itself.

World War I and Revolution

Whilst you are reading the story of Russia's part in World War One think about

- why Russia lost the war
- how defeat in war affected the Tsar's government.

In 1914 Russia entered the First World War on the side of Britain and France against Germany and Austria. The correspondent of The Times newspaper was in St Petersburg in July 1914 and has left this description of a demonstration held to greet the war.

A Extract from an article by the 'Times' correspondent, July 1914.

"

Before the Winter Palace, the great red house of the Tsars, stretches an enormous semicircle, which forms one of the greatest arenas in Europe. This is what we see now. More than 100,000 people of all classes and of all ranks standing for hours in the blazing sun before the building within which is their monarch. Quietly and orderly they wait, without hysteria and with the patience so characteristic of their race. At last the Tsar, moved by the magnitude of the demonstration, appears upon the balcony overlooking the square. Instantly the throng sinks upon its knees and with absolute spontaneity sings the deep-throated Russian anthem. For perhaps the first time since Napoleon's invasion of Russia the people and their Tsar were one, and the strength that unity spreads in a nation stirred throughout the Empire.

"

B Map showing Russian involvement in the First World War.

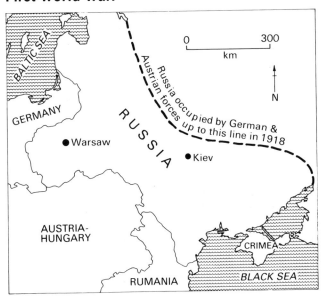

The German army defeated the Russian army at the Battle of Tannenberg (29 August 1914), where 90,000 Russian soldiers were taken prisoner, and many more drowned in the Masurian Lakes.

The military position got worse very quickly. General Balaiev reported from the Front to the Tsar in March 1915 that the army was running out of rifles.

Because things were going badly, the Tsar decided, in 1915, to go to the Front and take personal control of the war effort. This decision was a very important one for him. Some of his ministers did not want him to go because they knew he would be blamed if things went wrong. They were also worried that the Tsarina would be left to take charge of the Government. She was unpopular, partly because of her German birth.

They were right. The Tsarina fell increasingly under the influence of a man called Rasputin. He was a peasant who claimed to be a Holy Man. He had been introduced to the Tsar's family in 1905 and claimed that he could cure the Tsar's heir, Alexis, of his haemophilia. The alliance between Rasputin and the Tsarina was a disaster for Russia.

Many nobles were angry that Rasputin seemed to have the final say in the choice of ministers, dismissing good men and bringing in his own friends. Many of the town workers were angry that food supplies were running short. Rasputin was blamed for the hunger in the cities.

The Tsar's wife wrote letters to her husband whilst he was away commanding the armies at the Front

Questions

1 Read Source **A** and look back at the photograph of Nicholas blessing his troops on page 7.
   a How is the reaction of the Russian troops typical of the attitude of the Russian people to the Tsar?
   b Why, despite the problems which the Tsar had faced before 1914 did the people support him in this way on the occasion described in Source **A**?
2 Look at photograph **C** on the next page.
   a Who might have taken the photograph?
   b The photograph shows a young boy in the foreground. Why do you think the photographer chose to take a picture of a young boy?
3 What do you think? Were the Russian nobles right in wanting to get rid of Rasputin?

C Russian prisoners of war, May 1915.

in World War One. These tell us how the Government was run:

D Extracts from a letter from Tsarina Alexandra to her husband Tsar Nicholas.

"

Deary, I heard that that horrid Rodzianko (the leader of the Duma) wants the Duma to be called together – oh please don't, it's not their business, they want to discuss things not concerning them and bring more discontent – they must be kept away. . . .

No, hearken unto our Friend (Rasputin). He has your interest at heart – it is not for nothing God sent him to us – only we must pay attention to what he says. . . . Forgive me, but I don't like the choice of the Minister of War (General Polivanov). . . . is he not our Friend's enemy, as that brings bad luck. . . .

Now, before I forget, I must give you a message from our Friend, prompted by what he saw in the night (in a dream). He begs you to order that one should advance nearer Riga, says it is necessary, otherwise the Germans will settle down so firmly for the winter that it will cost endless bloodshed and trouble to make them move. . . .

"

When the Tsar's wife referred to 'autocratic Emperor' and 'constitutional government' (see Source **G** page 7) she was mentioning different ways in which Russia could be run. In the chapter on Tsar Nicholas (page 6) we saw that an autocrat was someone who had complete power over the country he ruled. In the chapter on 'Bloody Sunday' (page 12) we saw that Nicholas did not want to give up this power, because this would mean that he would be bringing in a type of 'constitutional government'. This would mean sharing power with an elected body like a Duma or parliament.

In late December 1916 Rasputin was murdered by a nobleman, but criticism of the Tsar did not stop. The war had brought many economic problems and sharp increases in food prices in big cities like Petrograd (St Petersburg) and Moscow.

On February 22, 1917 the Putilov engineering works in Petrograd closed down because of a lack of fuel. 40,000 workers lost their jobs and then decided to strike. They asked other workers to join them. Groups of women attacked bakeries because the bread queues had become too long.

The next day happened to be International Women Workers' Day. 90,000 people went on strike in Petrograd. Soldiers who had deserted from the army joined in the demonstrations and protests. It was clear that the war was having a very serious effect on the economy at home.

The next day almost 200,000 went on strike. Soldiers were on duty throughout the city of Petrograd to stop people moving around. However they did not want to open fire on the workers. Indeed when shops were looted on the following day the troops did not stop it. Some Cossacks even opened fire on the police.

E Letter from the Tsarina Alexandra to her husband, Tsar Nicholas II, 25 February 1917

"

The strikers and rioters in the city are now in a more defiant mood than ever. The disturbances are created by hoodlums. Youngsters and girls are running around shouting they have no bread; they do this just to create some excitement. If the weather were cold they would all probably be staying at home. But the thing will pass and quiet down, provided the Duma behaves. The worst of the speeches are not reported in the papers, but I think that for speaking against the dynasty there should be immediate and severe punishment.

"

F Grigory Efimovich Rasputin

train's progress was slow, he decided to return to army headquarters at Pskov and there his generals told him that the situation was hopeless. Russia was in revolution. He decided to abdicate in favour of his brother Michael and signed the decree of abdication on 2 March. However on the next day Michael refused to accept the crown.

A new temporary government, the Provisional Government, took over, and Kerensky eventually became its leader.

G The revolutionary leader Trotsky recalled:

> Every individual had his own people among the troops: a son, a husband, a brother, a relative. One met with soldiers now far oftener; saw them off to the front, lived with them when they came home on leave, chatted with them on the streets and in the tramways about the front, visited them in the hospitals.
>
> The workers' districts, the barracks, the front and, to an extent the villages too became communicating vessels. The workers would know what the soldiers were thinking and feeling. They had innumerable conversations about the war, about the people who were getting rich out of the war, about the generals, the governments, tzar and tzarina. The soldier would say about the war: To hell with it! And the worker would answer about the government: To hell with it!

Questions

4 Read Source **D**.
  a What is the Tsarina's attitude towards the Duma? Support your answer with a quote from the source.
  b How does her attitude to the Duma help explain why there was likely to be a revolution?
  c From reading this source, how much influence do you think Rasputin had over the governing of Russia and conduct of the war?
5 Who does the Tsarina (in Source **E**) think is causing disturbances in the streets, and how does this help explain why there was likely to be a revolution?

Questions

6 Documents **D** and **E** are letters written by the Tsarina. What are the advantages and disadvantages to the historian of using letters like this as evidence?
7 How does Source **G** show the writer's bias against the Tsar's government?

Follow-on questions

8 Some historians have said that it was a mistake for Nicholas II to go to the Front and take personal control of the war effort. Why do you think this was so?
9 This chapter gives a number of reasons why Russia began to lose the war. List those reasons and explain why they made revolution now more likely.
10 Was the revolution against the Tsar, in March 1917, planned or spontaneous? Explain your answer with reference to the sources.

On 27 February a regiment mutinied, killed its officers and paraded around Petrograd, calling on the people to take part in a revolution. Fighting broke out in many parts of the city.

On the morning of 28 February the Tsar travelled by train towards his palace at Tsarko Selo to join his wife and children. Because the

The Russian Revolution

This exercise deals with the events leading up to the first Russian Revolution of 1917. You will need to read the chapters so far again.

Questions

This exercise is about the *CAUSES* of the Russian Revolution. The *CAUSES* are the things that made the Revolution happen.

When we talk about the things that happened as a result of the *CAUSES*, we use the word *EFFECTS*. Look at how these terms are used in the following diagram:

CAUSES – 1. a piece of soap fell into the sink and covered the plug hole
↓

2. the tap was dripping because it needed a new washer
↓

3. the owner of the house went out for the day, not noticing that the sink was blocked
↓

EFFECT –   a flooded bathroom

1 *Making a list of causes.*
Re-read the sources about the Russian Revolution. As you look through them look for *causes*. Each time you think you might have found something that was a cause of the Revolution, write your idea down, then write down the source it came from, for example:
   'Nicholas disliked making decisions and above all he disliked saying disagreeable things to people'.

Do not go on to the next stage without completing this one carefully.

2 *Use your list of causes to answer the question: What were the five most important causes of the Russian Revolution? Give reasons for your choice, using detailed evidence from the sources.*

You should now have a long list of causes, it could be as many as 15. Some people may have more, others fewer.
Now you have to decide which was the most important cause, and why. For example, here are two possible causes of the Revolution:
a the personality of the Tsar
b the living conditions of the peasants.
Some people might say that cause **b** was more important than cause **a**, because millions of people lived in these terrible conditions. Others might say the opposite. The personality of the Tsar was more important because he had so much power and he could influence the way lots of people lived.

3 *Copy out the list you made in question 1 again, but this time* in order of importance. *Put what you think is the most important cause at the top. Think why you chose this as the most important cause.*

4 *When you have chosen your five most important causes, write a long paragraph (200 words) about each of them. Explain the reasons for your choice as carefully as you can. Back up your answer with short quotations. The best marks will be given for carefully thought out reasons. Remember to comment on the reliability of the sources. Do not take them at face value!*

You could write your ideas down like this:

Cause	Name of source
1. Nicholas' personality.	'Tsar Nicholas' Source **B** from 'Papa Tsar': Nicholas disliked making decisions and saying things which offended people.

The Provisional Government

While you are reading the information on the Provisional Government, think about:

a the problems which faced the Provisional Government in March, 1917,

b the mistakes they made in dealing with these problems,

c why it was Lenin and the Bolsheviks who succeeded them.

The main feature of the Revolution in March, 1917, was that it was not planned but took everyone by surprise. It had no leaders and, therefore, there was no one ready to take the leadership of the country. As a result, the leaders of the Duma were forced to take charge of the country. Prince G.E. Lvov became Prime Minister, and Paul Milyukov was Foreign Minister. The leader of the Petrograd (St Petersburg) Soviet, Alexander Kerensky, became Minister of Justice. This gave the Soviet some direct say in running the country. In effect, the Provisional Government and the Petrograd Soviet formed a 'Dual Government' which ruled Russia. Guchkov, the Minister of War, commented on this.

A Minister of War (Guchkov) on the power of the Provisional Government in March, 1917.

> The Provisional Government has no real force at its disposal, and its decrees are carried out only to the extent that is permitted by the Soviet of Workers and Soldiers' Deputies which has in its hands the most important elements of real power, the army, the railways, the post and telegraphs, etc. . . .

The Provisional Government had many important decisions to make, including:

1 What should happen to the ownership of land? They decided to leave it in the hands of its previous owners. As a result, scenes like the one illustrated here were common.

2 Whether or not to take Russia out of the war? Foreign Minister Milyukov was a strong supporter of the Allies, and pledged continued Russian involvement in the war. This meant that much-needed reform would have to be put off until after victory had been achieved.

Having said this, the Provisional Government did pass some very important reforms in its first few months. These included the introduction of an eight hour day, releasing political prisoners,

B Peasants looting a manor house.

Questions

1 Look at Source **B**.
   a Make a list of the items which are being taken from the manor house.
   b Why do you think the peasants acted in this way? Give reasons for your answer.

ending press censorship and abolishing capital punishment. Each of these measures was appreciated, but the main causes of the problems in Russian society remained.

Lenin made good use of these problems. He had been as surprised as anyone by the Revolution in March and was still in exile in Switzerland. The German government helped Lenin return to Petrograd in a 'sealed train' (from which no one was allowed to get on or off until it reached its destination) on April 16, because Lenin wanted Russia to make peace with Germany. This was one point in Lenin's 'April Theses' – his plans for the future of Russia should he and the Bolsheviks take control. Other important ideas were:

- Power should go to the Soviets who would control the country. This meant no support for the Provisional Government.
- The nationalisation of industry so that workers could control production.
- The state-ownership of land under the control of local Soviets and, therefore, the peasants.
- The improvement of food supplies to the towns

Lenin was going to give the peasants of Russia what they wanted: 'Peace', 'Bread', 'Land'.

C Extract from a speech by Lenin at the Finland Station,* 1917.

“

We don't need any parliamentary republic. We don't need any bourgeois democracy. We don't need any government except the Soviet of Workers', Soldiers' and Peasants' Deputies.

”

*Russian terminus stations take their names from the end of the line they serve.

The war was going from bad to worse for Russia. When Kerensky became Minister of War he decided that one major successful attack would boost the army's morale and unite the people. He was following a policy which had failed for the Tsar many years earlier, and the last ditch attack now led by General Brusilov was a failure for Kerensky also.

The 'July Days' followed in which many rank-and-file Bolsheviks took to the streets to demonstrate against the war, without the backing of Lenin and the other Bolshevik leaders. Without a clear plan, the revolt was easily crushed and many Bolsheviks were imprisoned, Lenin had to go into hiding in Finland.

However, Kerensky, who now led the Provisional Government, soon had to release the Bolsheviks because of the Kornilov affair. General Kornilov was Supreme Commander of the Russian Army and was worried about the threat of the Soviets:

D Extract from a speech by General Kornilov, 1917.

“

It is time to hang the German supporters and spies, with Lenin at their head, and to disperse the Soviet of Workers' and Soldiers' Deputies so that it can never reassemble.

”

General Kornilov attempted to set up a military dictatorship in September, 1917. However, he did not even reach Petrograd as he lacked the support of the people and even of some of his own troops. Kerensky had released the Bolsheviks, including Trotsky, to help defeat Kornilov.

The Bolsheviks now made plans with haste. They had a majority in the Petrograd Soviet now, and the problems were growing for Kerensky:

1 More and more troops were deserting from the army.
2 There were severe food shortages in the towns and bread queues were getting longer.
3 The factory workers were becoming restless, especially after hearing speeches made by Trotsky and other Bolsheviks.

Events were now working in the Bolsheviks' favour, and they laid careful plans to make the most of this opportunity. Events were master-minded by Lenin, with the very able assistance of Trotsky.

20 October: Lenin returned from exile to help Trotsky organise the final build-up to Revolution.

25 October: The Petrograd Soviet set up a Military Revolutionary Committee (MRC) to plan tactics.

3 November: The Petrograd Garrison supports the MRC.

5 November: Kerensky started his moves against the Bolsheviks, but it was too late.

6 November: The Red Guards took control of the major positions in the heart of Petrograd, including railway stations, bridges, power stations and the telephone exchange.

7 November: Kerensky left Petrograd as the Bolsheviks took over the rest of the city including the Winter Palace where the Provisional Government met.

When it came, the takeover of power by the Bolsheviks was quick and met with little resistance.

It was Trotsky who announced that the Provisional Government had been overthrown, and that the Bolshevik Revolution had succeeded. He was given the job of Commissar for Foreign Affairs and in 1918 negotiated a peace treaty at Brest-Litovsk with the Germans. The treaty brought the Soviet Union out of the war, but at terrible cost (huge areas of land were lost as we shall see in the next chapter).

E Offical Soviet painting: 'The First Word of the Soviet Government'.

Questions

2 Read Source **D**.
 a What is Kornilov suggesting about Lenin and the Soviet in this speech?
 b Why do you think he has done this?
 c Is this a reliable source of evidence about
  i Lenin and the Soviet?
  ii Kornilov?
  Explain your answers.
3 Draw a timeline and mark on it all of the important events involving the Provisional Government and the Bolsheviks between March and October, 1917.
4 Make a list of:
 a The problems which faced the Provisional Government in March, 1917.

 b How they dealt with these problems. How do these lists help explain why the Provisional Government fell from power in October, 1917?

Follow-on questions

5 Write a speech that might have been given by a Bolshevik to a group of workers in a Petrograd factory in September, 1917. In it, explain the failings of the Provisional Government, and why the Bolsheviks should be given the chance to rule the country.
6 How important was Lenin in the Bolshevik seizure of power? Explain your answer.

Lenin in power

As you read through this chapter, try to work out how Lenin made sure that the Bolsheviks stayed in power in the early months, and there was not a successful counter-revolution.

A A poster written by Lenin and issued immediately after the Revolution.

"

To the Citizens of Russia!

The Provisional Government has been deposed. State power has passed into the hands of the Petrograd Soviet of Workers' and Soldiers' Deputies – the Revolutionary Military Committee, which leads the Petrograd proletariat and the garrison.

The cause for which the people have fought, namely, the immediate offer of a democratic peace, the abolition of landed ownership, workers' control over production and the establishment of Soviet power – this cause has been secured.

Long live the revolution of workers, soldiers and peasants!

"

Questions

1 Study source A. What do the following words mean: deposed; proletariat; garrison?
2 Lenin promised the people of Russia 'Peace, Bread, Land'. Write out the phrases in the extract which are linked to these three words.

By 15 November, the Bolsheviks had taken control of Moscow. Elsewhere, if the Bolsheviks had control of the local Soviet they assumed overall power without much trouble. Other areas resisted the Bolsheviks.

But this was not the only problem which Lenin now faced. He had inherited the problems which had helped to bring down the Provisional Government. In addition, he was opposed by the Mensheviks, the Liberals, the Social Revolutionaries and the nobles, church and army officers who feared for their positions and wealth. Governments abroad were not very happy about these events either! Here is an example of the sort of anti-revolutionary propaganda which began to appear both in foreign newspapers and in journals published in Russia.

Lenin, unlike the Provisional Government, took quick and positive action. Elections were held for a Constituent Assembly or Parliament, with the following results:

B Cartoon by W.K. Haselden, published in the 'Daily Mail' in England in 1920.

IF WE ALL BECAME BOLSHEVISTS. . . .

Life would be conducted at the point of the pistol, by everybody against everybody else.

Votes Cast	
Social Revolutionaries	58%
Bolsheviks	25%
Mensheviks	4%
Others	13%
Number of Deputies	
Social Revolutionaries	370
Bolsheviks	175
Mensheviks	16
Others	146
Total	**707**

C The boundary changes made are a result of the Treaty of Brest-Litovsk, 1918.

Questions

3 Look at the cartoon (Source **B**) published in England.
  a What is the cartoonist suggesting that life would be like under a Bolshevik government in England?
  b What does this cartoon tell us about life in England in 1920?
  c In what ways is this cartoon biased?
4 The cartoon is biased. Does this mean that it is of no use to a historian of the Bolshevik Revolution? Explain your answer.

When it met, the Constituent Assembly lasted just one day. Red Guards then shut it down. Russia became a 'Dictatorship of the Proletariat'.

This was an indication of how the Bolsheviks would deal with opposition. Trotsky said in a reply to a Menshevik call for a coalition:

"
Your part is over. Go to the place where you belong from now on – the dustbin of history.
"

Lenin had promised 'Peace, Bread, Land'. The peasants had already taken possession of the land. The Communist Party of the Soviet Union (CPSU), as the Bolsheviks were now called, turned their attention to World War One. They made peace with Germany under the Treaty of Brest-Litovsk, signed in March, 1918. The peace terms were harsh. The Soviet Union lost 25% of its land area, about 30% of its population and 50% of its industry. Trotsky was the chief negotiator, and did not want to accept such terms as these. But Lenin argued that, without peace, the Revolution at home would be lost. He said that this territory could be reclaimed at a later date. He had learnt from the Provisional Government's mistake!

Opposition within the Soviet Union to the Bolshevik government continued, especially as the Constituent Assembly had been abolished. So the CPSU set up the Commission for Combating Sabotage and Counter-Revolution, or Cheka. Anyone who opposed the new government was imprisoned or executed.

D H.E. Salisbury's 'Russia in Revolution', 1978.

"
Lenin began more and more to invoke the doctrine of terror to strengthen his grip. While he had opposed its use as a revolutionary tactic, Lenin had always emphasized that terror was a fair weapon in the struggle of a revolutionary regime to consolidate and hold power.
"

Questions

5 How did Lenin justify the use of 'terror' in the period after the Revolution?
6 What does Source **D** tell us about Lenin?
7 Source **D** is a secondary source written by an historian some time after the Revolution. Does this mean that the evidence given about Lenin and his methods is unreliable? Explain your answer.

E Grain is stored in a church for distribution to workers in the towns.

Lenin did not have a 'magic wand' to produce more food for his people, however. Indeed, he sent groups of Communists into the countryside to seize grain from the peasants to feed the workers in the towns.

Other changes initially introduced by Lenin included the removal of land from the Orthodox Church, and forcing it to stop teaching religion. Women were also declared the social equals of men, and people were to call each other 'Comrade' or 'Citizen'.

Comparing these changes in a few months with what had happened under the Provisional Government, it becomes clear why the Communists held on to power in the early days. However, as Lenin had forseen, they were soon in the middle of a Civil War.

Questions

8 What do you think a church-goer and believer might have felt about the use of the church as a grain warehouse to feed the hungry people in the city?

9 Looking at this chapter as a whole.
   a Make a list of all of the problems which Lenin faced in October, 1917.
   b How did Lenin deal with these problems?

10 Now compare Lenin's policies with those of Kerensky. Do you think that Lenin had a better chance than Kerensky of keeping power in Russia? Give reasons for your answer.

11 Look at the map, Source C.
   Lenin moved the capital of the Soviet Union from Petrograd to Moscow after the Treaty of Brest-Litovsk. Can you explain why?

The Civil War 1918–21

As you read through this chapter, try to work out why, despite many disadvantages, the Communists (Reds) won the Civil War.

As we have seen, Lenin had many opponents in 1917 and did not control the whole of Russia. In 1918, Civil War broke out as these various opposition groups (the 'Whites') joined forces to try to overthrow the Communists (the 'Reds').

Led by Tsarist officers, the White armies contained Liberals, Social Revolutionaries, Mensheviks, richer peasants who wanted to keep their land, and national minority groups who wanted independence from Russia itself. In addition, the Allies, angered by Russia's desertion from the war, her preaching of world Communism and the cancellation of all debts of Tsarist Russia, sent troops and supplies to help the White armies.

A Map showing the two sides in the Civil War, 1918.

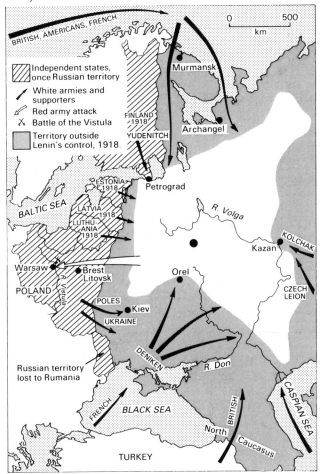

The war turned into a savage and bloody struggle. Despite their initial advantage, it soon became clear that the Whites were at a disadvantage for the following reasons:

a Their forces were scattered and were unable, and often unwilling, to act together.

b The peasants disliked both sides, but did not want the Whites to win because it would probably mean that they would lose their land. Therefore, they supported the Reds.

c The help of Russia's former allies to the Whites enabled the Reds to appeal to the patriotism of the Russian people, because foreigners were invading their land.

d The foreign troops were not very determined as they did not sympathise with either side.

e The brilliance of Trotsky in leading the Red Army.

The Civil War was really a series of battles, uncoordinated with each other.

General Kolchak attacked first in the east in the spring of 1919. Within a few weeks he reached Kazan (see Source **A**), but by summer, Kolchak's forces were in retreat. This continued until the following February when Kolchak was captured and shot.

General Deniken launched his main attack in the late spring of 1919. By June his forces had reached the Volga (see Source **A**), but progress then became slower. By October he was still at least 300 kilometres from Moscow. At this point, with Kolchak almost defeated, Trotsky poured men and munitions into the battle against Deniken. By mid-December, Kiev (see Source **A**) fell to the Reds and Deniken was retreating fast. By March 1920, Deniken had resigned his command, and his troops had either fled or joined those of General Wrangel.

General Yudenitch attacked from the north in the late spring and early summer of 1919. With Trotsky dealing with Deniken's advance in the south, Yudenitch had an easy march to the outskirts of Petrograd. However, he failed to

Questions

1 Study the map.
   a Describe the position of the Red Army in the summer of 1918.
   b What disadvantages did it have at this time?
   c What advantages, if any, did it have?
   d Which side do you think had the best chance of winning the war at the start? Explain your answer by referring to the map.

B A Communist cartoon showing the White Armies fleeing at the end of the Civil War.

capture the city because he could not block the Bolshevik supply lines. By the end of the year, Yudenitch's army was in tatters, and defeated.

In late April, 1920, a surprise attack came from Poland. The Poles hoped to regain land lost to Russia in the past, and capture Kiev by early May. The Bolshevik counter-attack pushed them back, however, and they agreed a peace in October 1920, having gained very little from the expedition.

The final threat to the Reds came from General Wrangel in June 1920. He regrouped Deniken's forces, and launched another attack from the south. However, any hopes he may have had were dashed when the Poles made peace in October, as Trotsky now only had to deal with Wrangel. His White forces finally withdrew in mid-November 1920.

Trotsky was able to defeat these attacks one by one. He went from one front to another in a special train as his campaign headquarters. Each time he spoke to the troops and encouraged them to fight just that little bit harder. Lenin said of Trotsky at this time:

> Could anyone point out to me another man who would organise an almost model army in a year and win the respect of military experts? We have such a man.

The members of the Red Army had the will to win, not least because they were fighting for their own futures and their ownership of land. As each battle was won, so the Communists kept control of that area and brought it under Soviet rule. War

Questions

2 a Who is pulling the cart?
  b Why are the Generals shown on the ground behind the cart?
3 a Why do you think the cartoonist has put top hats on the people riding on the cart?
  b What is the grass made of? Why do you think the cartoonist has drawn the grass in this way?
4 Is this a fair summary of the events of the Civil War? Explain your answer.

with Poland delayed the inevitable Red victory, but the Treaty of Riga, signed in March 1921, brought an end to the war in the west. Japan had joined in the Civil War on the side of the Whites to try to destroy their joint enemy, the Communists. Japan was finally defeated in the east in 1922. The whole of Russia was now a Communist country.

During the War, Lenin had been forced to introduce the economic policy known as 'War Communism'. His main aim was to keep the Red Army supplied and fed. To do this he had to turn the whole of Russia into a forced labour camp. Industry was controlled by the government, and crops were seized without payment. No trade was alllowed, except by the government. This policy succeeded in its aim of keeping the Red Army going, but it had a disastrous effect on the people of Russia. Factories stopped producing and peasants burned their crops rather than give them to the government.

C The effects of World War, Revolution and Civil War on Russian industrial and agricultural production.

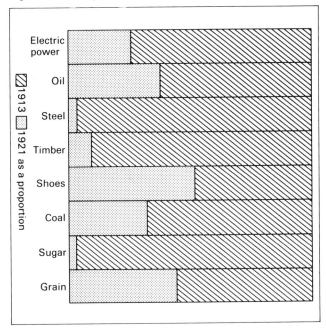

For the people, the result was famine in which, in 1921, 5 million people are estimated to have died. An eye-witness described the situation.

D Eye-witness account of the famine in Russia in 1921.

"

Winter was a torture for the townspeople: no heating, no lighting and the ravages of famine. Children and feeble old folk died in their thousands. Typhus was carried everywhere by lice... Inside Petrograd's grand apartments, now abandoned, people were crowded in one room, lived on top of one another around a little stove which would be standing on the floor, its flue belching smoke through an opening in the window. Fuel for it would come from the floorboards of rooms nearby, from the last sticks of furniture available, or else from books. Entire libraries disappeared in this way... People dined on a pittance of oatmeal, or half-rotted horsemeat, a lump of sugar would be divided into tiny fragments among a family, and a single mouthful taken out of turn would start angry scenes. The local Commune did everything it could to keep the children fed, but what it managed was pitiful.

"

In March, 1921, discontent flared up when a section of the Red Army mutinied at the Kronstadt naval base on the Baltic. These sailors had been some of the first supporters of the Bolsheviks. Now they were objecting to the increasing dictatorship of Lenin and his government.

Trotsky managed to put down the mutiny, but Lenin was now in no doubt that a change of policy was needed. He said: 'We are in a condition of such poverty, ruin and exhaustion... that everything must be set aside to increase production.'

He therefore introduced the New Economic Policy (NEP). This was a step back from the harshness of War Communism, and introduced some Capitalist ideas alongside the Communist ones. Small industries could be privately owned, and peasants could sell their surplus harvest after they had given up a previously agreed amount of grain to the government. Private trade became legal again, and a new coinage was issued to restore the value of money. Heavy industry, transport and foreign trade remained in the hands of the government.

This was, indeed. a move away from Communism, allowing private trade for private profit. However, it was only introduced as a temporary measure and the next few years were to show that Lenin had made the right decision. By 1928 output had reached its 1914 level, which showed that the Russian economy was on the road to recovery, even though they were a long way behind the countries of Western Europe and America.

Questions

5 Look back through this chapter.
   a What do you think was the most important reason why the Whites lost the Russian Civil War?
   b Give reasons for your answer to 4a by comparing it to other causes of the Whites' defeat.
6 You are a foreign visitor to Russia in 1921. Describe your experiences as you travel through the country, mentioning the views of the people you talk to on the way. Points to include:
   a Lenin and the Communist Party
   b Trotsky and the Red Army
   c the White Armies
   d the famine
   Remember, not everyone would have the same opinions!

Lenin's last days, 1923–24

As you read through the information and sources in this chapter and the next, try to work out:
- who Lenin wanted to succeed him as leader of the USSR;
- why it was Stalin, not Trotsky, who won the struggle.

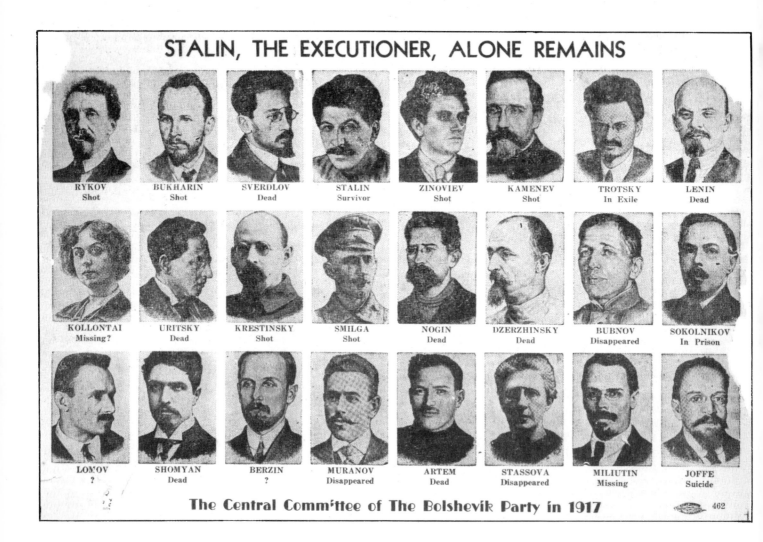

STALIN, THE EXECUTIONER, ALONE REMAINS

RYKOV Shot	BUKHARIN Shot	SVERDLOV Dead	STALIN Survivor	ZINOVIEV Shot	KAMENEV Shot	TROTSKY In Exile	LENIN Dead
KOLLONTAI Missing?	URITSKY Dead	KRESTINSKY Shot	SMILGA Shot	NOGIN Dead	DZERZHINSKY Dead	BUBNOV Disappeared	SOKOLNIKOV In Prison
LOMOV ?	SHOMYAN Dead	BERZIN ?	MURANOV Disappeared	ARTEM Dead	STASSOVA Disappeared	MILIUTIN Missing	JOFFE Suicide

The Central Committee of The Bolshevik Party in 1917

462

A 'Lenin's General Staff of 1917' – a newspaper 'gallery' published in the USA in the 1930's by followers of Leon Trotsky.

Lenin made a will before he died. In this document he set out his hopes and fears for the new Soviet Union that would grow up after his death. Lenin was very ill after a terrible stroke and did not have long to live. He wrote down what he thought about Stalin and Trotsky. This will is called Lenin's 'Political Testament':

B From Lenin's 'Political Testament' written in late 1922.

"

Comrade Stalin, having become General Secretary has concentrated enormous power in his hands; and I am not sure that he has always known how to use that power with sufficient caution. On the other hand comrade Trotsky is, to be sure, the most able man in the present central committee – but is also too self-confident.

"

C From a postscript to Lenin's 'Political Testament', added on 4 January 1923.

" Stalin is too rude, and this . . . becomes insupportable in the office of a general secretary. Therefore, I propose to the comrades to find a way to remove Stalin from the position and appoint to it another man who will be more patient, more loyal, more polite and more considerate to comrades. "

In January 1924 Lenin suffered another stroke and died. The terrible news was brought to Trotsky far in the south of the country, where he had gone to rest and recover from malaria. Trotsky immediately telegraphed to the Kremlin 'I think it is necessary to return to Moscow. When is the funeral?' An hour later the reply reached him. It had been sent by Stalin: 'The funeral will take place on Saturday 26. You will not be able to return on time.' In fact it took place on the Sunday – so Trotsky could have returned in time – and it was Stalin, not Trotsky, who was photographed leading the mourners. It was Stalin, not Trotsky, who gave the funeral speech praising Lenin – the man who had suggested Stalin's 'removal'.

It was Stalin, and not Trotsky, who was to follow Lenin and eventually become leader of the Soviet Union. It was a slow victory, not a dramatic, sudden one. Although Lenin died in 1924, Stalin did not really become known and established in public as leader until about four years later.

Lenin had been warned about Stalin in the two years immediately before his death. During the Civil War, Stalin increased his power. He was sent down to Tsaritsyn (later renamed Stalingrad) to organise food supplies. However, he soon began to run the whole area as a political dictator, even changing Trotsky's orders. Lenin put up with him because he was doing the job required (he was getting supplies moving). Once the Civil War had been won Stalin went back to his old job as Commissar of Nationalities and used his power to crush with great violence a rebellion in his home state of Georgia. Lenin ordered him to stop using so much force, but Stalin ignored these orders.

In early 1922 Stalin became Secretary-General of the Central Committee of the Communist Party. Whilst Lenin was alive this was not considered to be a very important post. However, it could be used to manipulate events in favour of its holder. The Secretary-General controlled appointments to all levels of the party. This meant that Stalin could decide who got the important jobs. Stalin put his supporters into key positions in central and local government. It is interesting to note that it was Trotsky, among others, who suggested that Stalin be given this and other jobs that were thought to be boring administrative posts.

Now look at the next chapter to find out how the Struggle for Power ended and what happened to Trotsky.

Questions

1 In what way could Source **A** be described as biased against Stalin? Support your answer with quotations from Source **A**.
2 Read Sources **B** and **C**.
  a What complaints does Lenin make against Stalin?
  b Is Lenin suggesting that Trotsky should become leader after him?
  c Are these Sources biased? Explain your answer.

Follow-on question

3 Source **A** was put together by Trotsky's followers in America in the 1930's
  a Why do you think it was made?
  b What sources of evidence might we use to check the claims made in Source **A**?
  c Source **A** is biased against Stalin. Does that mean it is useless as evidence to the historian of the Struggle for Power? Explain your answer.

The struggle for power

Stalin had insulted Lenin's wife, so she wanted Lenin's 'Testament' to be published. However, Stalin convinced Trotsky that it was not in the best interests of the country to publish the will. After all, it had not exactly been full of praise for Trotsky. It gives clues about why Trotsky wasn't very popular amongst other Politburo members.

The struggle for power was in some ways a struggle of ideas – between Trotsky's 'left' ideas – called 'Permanent Revolution' – and Stalin's policy of 'Socialism in one country'.

'Socialism in one country' stated that the first priority should be to build up Soviet strength and make her self-sufficient, even if this involved a small amount of capitalism at first. Then the USSR would be in a better position to help promote Communist revolutions in other countries.

The 'Permanent Revolution' idea was based on an immediate return to full Communism at home (instead of the New Economic Policy) and the promotion of Communist revolutions abroad. It was felt that the success of these revolutions abroad would protect the Russian Revolution.

Trotsky's ideas were so important to him that he published a book in 1924 'Lessons of October' in which he criticised Zinoviev and Kamenev, two other Politburo members.

A Trotsky's criticism of his rival.

> Stalin is a past master of the art of tying a man to him, not by winning his admiration but by forcing him into committing terrible and unforgivable crimes. These are the bricks of the pyramid of which Stalin is the top.

Stalin had 'tied' Zinoviev and Kamenev to him and the three men plotted to strip Trotsky of all his power. In 1925 he was appointed to serve on the Supreme Economic Council.

Trotsky was forced to resign from the Politburo in 1926. Later he was expelled from the Party and went into the political wilderness: first into internal exile to Alma Ata on the Chinese border, and then exiled from the USSR itself.

Unfortunately for Zinoviev and Kamenev, once they had helped remove Trotsky from the Politburo they were no longer of any value to Stalin. Soon they were expelled from the Party and, eventually, as we shall see, were put on trial.

Alas poor Trotsky! The man described as 'the greatest Jew since Jesus Christ' spent the 1930's wandering from country to country until in 1940

he met the final moment of destiny described in the newspaper Source **B**.

 DAILY NEWS

Vol. 22. No. 50   New York, Thursday, August 22, 1940.   60 Pages   2 Cents

TROTSKY IS DEAD

Story on Page 2

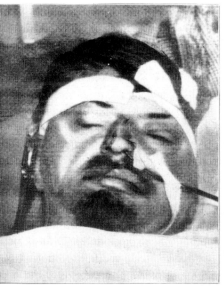

↑ Trotsky Death Weapon
Mexican policemen show short-handled pickax with which Frank Jackson fatally wounded the exiled Leon Trotsky, military genius of the Russian Revolution. Jackson, beaten by police, is recovering in hospital where Trotsky died. —Story p. 2.

← Dying, He Blamed Stalin
In pain-wracked hours of his battle for life in Mexico City hospital, Trotsky knew death was coming, and said: "Stalin has finally accomplished the task he unsuccessfully attempted before."

(Wide World Wired foto)

B Front page of an American newspaper, August 22nd, 1940.

Questions

1 What were the main events of the struggle for power from 1918 to 1940? Write your answer in the form of a timeline.

2 **a** Look back at Trotsky's biography (page 21). What do you think his strengths were? And his weaknesses?

   b What mistakes do you think he made in the struggle for power? Support your explanation with quotations. Use evidence from 'Lenin's Last Days' too.

3 In the chapter on Stalin you noted down what sort of a person you thought he was and what his strengths were. How did he use these strengths to win the struggle for power? Support your explanation by quoting things he did. Use evidence from the 'Lenin's Last Days' chapter as well.

Collectivisation: theory

Use the sources in this chapter to help you understand:

a why Stalin introduced Collectivisation;
b what problems he faced;
c how big the changes were for the peasants.

Once Stalin had won the struggle for power and become leader of the Soviet Union he set about making changes that were to affect all his people.

In a speech in 1931 he looked back to Russia's history and explained that a new policy was needed.

A Speech by Stalin, 1931

"
The history of the old Russia has consisted in being beaten again and again . . . because of her . . . backwardness, military backwardness, industrial backwardness, agricultural backwardness. She was beaten because to beat her has paid off and because people have been able to get away with it. If you are backward and weak then you are in the wrong and may be beaten and enslaved. But if you are powerful . . . people must beware of you. We are fifty to a hundred years behind the advanced countries. We must make up this gap in ten years. Either we do this or they crush us.
"

Questions

1 Quote evidence from Source **A** to show that Stalin was trying to appeal to:
   a Communists
   b all Russians, not just Communists.
2 Political speeches are given for particular reasons. What do you think was Stalin's aim or purpose in giving this speech (Source **A**)?
3 Copy these statements and then explain whether you think they are true or false. Quote figures from Source **B** to support your answer.
   a The Soviet economy was in a mess in 1928.
   b The Soviet economy was recovering in 1928.
   c You can't trust figures.
4 Name any two other sources of evidence which might help you judge how well the Soviet economy was doing in 1928. Explain your answer.

It would not be easy to catch up so much ground so quickly. Between 1914 and 1921 the country had been through a World War, two revolutions and a Civil War. The economic problems facing the Soviet Union can be seen in this table:

B Soviet production in agriculture and industry, 1913, 1916 and 1921.

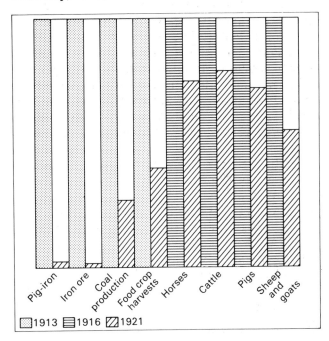

Lenin had wanted to make the Soviet Union a Socialist country. This would mean that factories, banks, businesses and land would be taken over by the government and private property would be banned. The problem was that over 80% of the population were peasants who did not seem to want to give up the land they had taken from the nobles during the revolution.

The peasants had violently resisted Lenin's policy of War Communism (page 32). The New Economic policy (N.E.P.) was only a short term measure. It was not a socialist idea.

Lenin had died in 1924 without his socialist dream coming true. Stalin wanted to become Communism's second Lenin and lead the country to new achievements which would be as important to the Soviet Union as the Bolshevik Revolution of 1917.

So Stalin set about building '*Socialism in one country*'. To do this he announced a series of targets to be reached in five years for the modernisation of agriculture and industry. The aims of the 'Five Year Plan' which began in 1928 can be seen in Source **D** on the next page.

C A group of peasants harvesting in 1923.

D Official Soviet poster, 1929, describing the aims of the Five Year Plan for steel smelting. The USSR (CCCP) will overtake England.

If the Plan was to be successful, then agriculture and industry would have to work together for socialism, Stalin explained in 1929.

E Speech by Stalin in 1929.

"

There are two ways of doing this. There is the capitalist way, which is to make the peasants poor and set up capitalist businesses in farming. We reject this way as it does not fit in with the Soviet economic system. There is a second way: the Socialist way, which is to set up collective farms and state farms. This way leads to the small farms being grouped into large collective farms, technically and scientifically equipped. The capitalist elements will be squeezed out of agriculture. We are in favour of this second way.

"

Questions

5 a What does Source **D** tell us about Stalin's aims for the Five Year Plan?

  b Why is Britain shown in Source **D**? Explain your answer and support it with evidence from Source **A**.

6 Look at Source **C**.

  a Does it prove that agriculture was inefficient in the USSR in 1923?

  b Sources of evidence may be understood differently by different people. How might Source **C** be used by (*i*) supporters of Stalin? (*ii*) opponents of Collectivisation?

7 Copy these statements and then explain whether they are true or false.

  a Source **D** is a reliable source of evidence about Soviet production figures.

  b Source **D** is a reliable source of evidence about Soviet propaganda.

8 Look at your answers to question 7. How can a source be both reliable and unreliable?

9 Why did Stalin bring in the policy of Collectivisation? Source **E** will help you.

F Comment by a British historian on the method of Collectivisation, 1929:

"

But what was 'collectivisation'? No-one had prepared for it; no army of experts had worked out what to do with 120 million bewildered peasants.

As the orders were sent to local party leaders to carry out collectivisation, only one thing was clear: the peasants of a village must pool their land and their equipment and work in future under the orders of a collective farm committee over which the Party would keep a tight control. But no other details were given: it was left unclear whether a collective should pay its workers 'by eaters' (according to the number of mouths in a worker's family), according to the work they did, or according to the tools they contributed. In some areas peasants were allowed to keep their livestock: in others, the cows, pigs, sheep, goats, horses and chickens were all collectivised.

"

Some peasants were not in favour of Collectivisation. They did not want to give away their strips of land or use the new machinery. The Communist Party sent officials to the farms to tell the peasants about the benefits of the new system.

G Speech made by a Communist in 1929.
(Reported by an American who had returned to his family village in the Soviet Union.)

"

I suppose they have been shedding tears about the Kolkhoz, he said . . . Tell me, you wretched people, what hope is there for you if you remain on individual pieces of land? From year to year as you increase in population you divide and sub-divide your strips of land. You cannot even use machinery on your land because no machine man ever made could stand the rough ridges that the strip system creates. You will have to work in your own way and stew in your old misery. Don't you see that under your present system there is nothing ahead of you but ruin and starvation?

You accuse us of making false promises . . . last year you got a schoolhouse, and have you forgotten how we of the Party and of the Soviet had to squeeze out of you through the voluntary tax your share of the cost of the schoolhouse? And now? Aren't you glad your children can attend school? . . . Were we wrong when we urged you to build a fire station? Were we wrong when we urged you to lay decent bridges across your stream in the swamp? Were we wrong when we threatened to fire you if you didn't take home two loads of peat to mix with the bedding for your stock so as to have good fertiliser? . . .

The Kolkhoz is different, shouted the old man . . . Of course it is different. If we didn't believe in making things different, we never would have overthrown the Tsar and the capitalists and the landlords . . . Different? Of course, but better.

Don't you see? Isn't it about time you stopped thinking each one for himself and for his own piggish hide? You *Kulaks* of course will never become reconciled to a new order. You love to fatten on other people's blood. But we know how to deal with you. We'll wipe you off the face of the earth.

"

Questions

10 a Make a full list of the problems Stalin faced in Collectivisation. Try to make your list as full as possible.
b Look at your list and note those things that involved a lot of *change*.
c Rearrange your list into priority order, with the most difficult at the top and the least difficult at the bottom.
d Add sentences to your four most difficult items, saying *why* you think them so difficult, using quotations from the sources.

H Russian peasants examining a new tractor.

Collectivisation: practice

This chapter describes how Collectivisation changed life in the villages. Work out:
- How did the government want Collectivisation to be seen and understood?
- What were conditions for the peasants really like?
- How far can we trust the sources of evidence about Collectivisation?

By February 1930 the Government claimed that half of all Soviet peasants had joined collective farms. By July 1932 the figure had gone up to 62%. This massive change had been made in less than three years. However, not all peasants were welcome on the new farms.

A Extract of speech by Stalin in December, 1929:

66

We have passed to the policy of eliminating the Kulaks as a class. . . . To launch an attack against the Kulaks means that we must prepare for it and then strike at the Kulaks, strike so hard as to prevent them from rising to their feet again.'

99

Kulaks who were thought to be 'actively hostile' to the Government were rounded up by the secret police. Many were sent to prison camps in remote parts of the Soviet Union such as Siberia. Others just disappeared and were never heard of again. The French historian, Professor Sorlin, has written that at least 3 million of about 4½ million Kulaks died as a result of being sent to these camps. The problem is that we haven't got accurate figures of the numbers, and we do not know exaclty what happened to them, so we have to rely on the eye-witness accounts of people who lived in the Soviet Union at that time and wrote about what they saw.

Victor Serge was a French communist. He described how lots of peasants refused to co-operate with the authorities:

C Extract from 'Memoirs of a Revolutionary 1901–41' by Victor Serge (1963).

66

In a market town the whole population was deported (sent away). The women undressed in their houses, thinking that nobody would dare to make them go naked; they were driven out as they were to the cattle trucks, beaten with rifle butts. Train loads of deported peasants left for the icy north, the forest, the steppes and the deserts. These were whole populations, who had lost everything; the old folk starved to death in mid-journey, new-born babies were buried on the banks of the roadside, and each wilderness had its crop of little crosses of white wood. Other populations, dragging all their mean possessions on wagons rushed towards the borders of Poland, Romania and China, crossed them by no means intact, to be sure – in spite of the machine guns.

99

B Government photograph of peasants crowding to learn about Collectivisation.

Motor Tractor Stations were set up at important regional centres, to supply tractors. It was an enormous job, because the peasants had previously worked only with hand tools.

At first the peasants had problems repairing broken tractors. However within a few years some of the peasants had learned the necessary skills and more of the machinery was in working order. The new system involved a complete change in the way of life, with a far greater need to work together, rather than just look after yourself.

The harvest failed in 1932 and a halt was called to Collectivisation. At least 5½ million peasants starved to death when Soviet officials seized grain stocks from the peasants.

D The effect Collectivisation on the Soviet Union.

Grain harvests and state demands

(*in million of tonnes*)

	1928	1929	1930	1931	1932	1933
Grain harvest	73.3	71.7	83.5	69.5	69.6	68.4
State grain demands	10.8	16.1	22.1	22.8	18.5	22.6

Livestock (*million head*)

	1928	1929	1930	1931	1932	1933
Cattle	70.5	67.1	52.5	47.9	40.7	38.4
Pigs	26.0	20.4	13.6	14.4	11.6	12.1
Sheep and goats	146.7	147.0	108.8	77.7	52.1	50.2

E Peasants looking at a government poster, showing a Kulak or overseer (right) and a peasant (left).

F An illiteracy liquidation class.

Questions

1 Explain how Collectivisation changed life in the village. List the main changes.

2 a Describe each photograph in detail.

  b How far can we trust them as evidence about life on collective farms in the 1930's? Explain your answer.

3 a Make a list of the various methods the Communist Party used to try to make sure that Collectivisation was introduced effectively throughout the country.

  b Does the fact that they had to use these methods mean that Collectivisation was a mistake? Explain your answer.

4 Many of these photographs and those in other history books show the 'government view' of Collectivisation. Why do you think there aren't many photographs showing 'bad' sides of collectivised farms?

Stalin and Industrialisation

This is a coursework exercise in which you will be using the evidence and information from this chapter to help you work out how Stalin's industrial policies changed the Soviet Union.

You will need to remember the two ideas of change and continuity. This means that you will need to be aware that some things can remain the same while others change quickly.

Before you start it is worth remembering that you will have to look at the evidence in a critical way. Think about:

a What the evidence is;
b Who made it;
c When the evidence was made;
d Why the evidence was made.

As you read through the information and sources try to work out:

- Why Stalin wanted to industrialise the Soviet Union so quickly.
- How he went about it.
- How the Soviet people felt about the methods he used.
- How successful Stalin's industrialisation policy was.

When we looked at Collectivisation we saw that Stalin believed that the USSR was '50 or 100 years behind the advanced countries.' He said 'We must make up this gap in ten years. Either we do this or they crush us.'

The Soviet Union was producing only 10% of the coal produced by Britain, and 6% of the amount produced by USA. Oil production was 50% of the British total but only 12% of the USA.

In the past Russian industry had been helped by the supply of machinery, money and experts from western countries. However in Stalin's time there was less of this help.

Stalin wanted to reorganise the planning of the economy so as to cope with the massive task of modernising his country. In 1921 Lenin had created an organisation called GOSPLAN (State Planning Commission). Its job was to estimate how much industry and agriculture would produce and how much profit they would make. Unfortunately this way of planning the economy did not work very well because the Civil War brought famine in the Soviet Union. Lenin had to allow private trade (see the section on N.E.P. page 33).

A **Production targets and achievements for the first Five Year Plan** (The first plan was stopped after four years, and the second one started.)

Industry	1927–28 production	Target for 1933	1932 production
Electricity (*milliard kWh*)	5.05	17.0	13.4
Coal (*million tonnes*)	35.4	68.0	64.3
Oil (*million tonnes*)	11.7	19.0	21.4
Steel (*million tonnes*)	4.0	8.3	5.9

Stalin changed GOSPLAN's purpose in 1927. He ordered GOSPLAN to produce targets which industry and agriculture would have to meet in different parts of the country. This was the way in which quick change was to be forced through. The targets were to be met at all costs. Orders went out from the capital about how towns, factories and industrial plants were to meet the targets. These targets were called Five Year Plans, as they had to be achieved in five years. Source **A** shows the targets and gives us an idea about how successfully they were met. The first plan concentrated on the build up of heavy industry, like coal, steel etc.

Overnight success was difficult to bring about. Stalin had to fight against old habits and problems, as we see in this description by an English visitor to the new industrial town of Magnitogorsk.

Questions

1 The first two Five Year Plans concentrated on heavy industry like oil and coal rather than consumer goods like shoes, clothing etc. Why do you think Stalin did this?
2 From what you know about the type of country Stalin was building, why do you think the capitalist countries would want to smash it?

B Description of Magnitogorsk by an English visitor.

"

The shortage of workers was made worse by the large loss of working time because of the old Russian custom of just not coming to work either on the morning after a drinking session, or simply because he did not feel like it. This was fought against but never completely beaten. Another cause of loss of working time was bad organisation of the workers. Two brigades of workers would be given a job where only one could work at a time. A brigade would be sent to pour concrete foundations before the digging work was finished. Workers would be sent to a job for which there were no materials or for which important tools or plans were not ready.

"

Lots of foreigners came to help out with the new work of building 'Socialism in one country', but it was still hard to buy machines if the capitalist world would not trade with the Soviet Union.

A huge education programme was started. Schools were even set up in factories. Women were vital to the workforce of the new Soviet Union. They did all sorts of skilled jobs that were not yet open to many women in the West – where a woman's place was still thought to be in the home. Besides working on building sites and in factories, women worked as doctors, dentists, teachers, lawyers and a host of other jobs. However the men and women of Stalin's Russia couldn't learn the new industrial skills overnight.

Stalin was ready to try anything to reach his industrial targets. He ordered boards to be put up outside the factories, showing the targets to be reached.

Those workers who reached the highest targets were rewarded with medals, and better pay, housing and holidays. Their names were put up on the 'honour boards' for everyone to see. One man, Alexei Stakhanov, managed to lead a well organised team of miners and cut 102 tons of coal in a single shift.

Even in successful capitalist countries like Germany it was thought difficult to cut more than 10 tons in a shift. Stakhanov was used by Stalin as a sort of model that workers were supposed to copy. If they worked together as a team then they too could be 'Stakhanovites' – and be successful and maybe just a little rich!

So Stalin used some methods which many Socialists would not approve of. He offered the workers incentives, or rewards, for working hard.

C Workers at the new industrial town of Magnitogorsk studying a board showing the overall general work plan of industrial construction work for September 1930.

Questions

3 a Describe some of the problems Stalin faced in trying to increase industrial production.
  b Why do you think Stalin offered his workers rewards?
4 a What do you think Stalin wanted workers who saw Source **C** to think and do?
  b Source **C** looks as if it has been 'posed'. Does this mean that it is unreliable as evidence to the historian of Stalin's industrialisation policy? Explain your answer.

D **Village house in Komensk in the Ukraine now kept as a 'museum'.**

Life in the new towns was very different from the old ways of the country. Many of the houses had electricity, running water, central heating and simple, plain furniture. Others lived in houses like the one in Source **D**.

E **Description of living conditions in an new industrial town of Magnitogorsk by the English visitor in the early 1930's.**

"

The roofs were usually made of old scrap metal, sometimes covered by sod or by thatch. The same house was inhabited by the family, the chickens, the pigs and the cow, if there was one. This was usual in the poorer sections of the Russian countryside. For these labourers the possession of chickens and goats was witness of the fact that they were 'living well' by the standards of Russian peasants . . . Magnitogorsk had ten theatres with a total seating capacity of 9,000, all attached to various clubs. The activities of these clubs were varied, and included drama classes, chess, art and reading groups.

"

However, some people didn't fit in with the new system. People were fined and punished for bad work. Others lost out in the queue for housing. When targets weren't reached it was often 'saboteurs' or 'wreckers' who got the blame. Many refused to co-operate with the new system and suffered the same fate as the Kulaks – they were sent to Gulags (labour camps).

F **An eyewitness describes the work the people from these camps did.**

"

At the end of the workday there were corpses left on the work site. The snow powdered their faces. One of them was hunched over beneath an overturned wheel-barrow; he had hidden his hands in his sleeves and frozen to death in that position. Someone had frozen with his head bent down between his knees. Two were frozen back to back leaning against each other . . . At night the sledges went out and collected them . . . And in the summer bones remained from corpses which had not been removed in time, and together with the shingle they got into the concrete of the last lock at the city of Belomorsk* and will be preserved there forever.

"

*Belomorsk was a city along the White Sea Canal, which was built on Stalin's orders.

44

G A dam under construction at Dneiprostroi as part of the development of hydro-electric power in the Soviet Union.

H The completed dam at Dneiprostroi.

Questions

5 Look at Source **D**. What evidence is there in the photograph to suggest that the people are
  a poor
  b unhealthy?
6 What do you think the hut in Source **D** was built out of, and why?
7 Look at Sources **G** and **H**.
  a What methods are being used to construct the dam?
  b What effect do you think the dam would have had on people's lives once it was operating?
  c How big do you think Stalin's industrial changes were? Write a long paragraph. Remember that you gain marks for selecting relevant information from the sources.
8 'Stalin's industrial policies changed the Soviet Union for the better.' Do these sources show this view to be true? Explain your answer in another long paragraph, with relevant quotations.

The Purges

This chapter describes the steps taken by Stalin to rid himself of his opponents. Whilst looking at the sources think about:

- what life was like for an opponent of Stalin during these years
- what the cost to the country was of these policies.

Stalin's policies of Collectivisation and Industrialisation had brought massive changes to the Soviet economy in just a few years. However between 1935 and 1939 Stalin introduced equally dramatic changes to the political life of the Soviet Union. These changes were known as the 'purges'. When you 'purge' something you get rid of it. Stalin 'got rid of' huge numbers of the Soviet people during this time. Some were put on trial and shot. Others were sent to forced labour camps. Others just disappeared and were never heard of again. It wasn't just important people in the government, civil service and army who suffered. Millions of people from the countryside and towns became victims of the purges. We'll never know exactly how many people died, but it was as if Stalin had declared war on his own people.

The purges are said to have begun after the murder of Sergei Kirov on 1 December 1934. Kirov was chairman of the Leningrad Soviet, and had been one of Stalin's closest supporters on the Politburo. Two of Stalin's old rivals, Zinoviev and Kamenev got the blame. They were arrested, along with a large number of people living in the Leningrad area. In the early 1920's Zinoviev and Kamenev had been more famous in the Soviet Union than Stalin. Many people thought that they had a better chance than Stalin of taking power when Lenin died. However, as we have seen, Stalin managed to convince Zinoviev and Kamenev to help him push Trotsky out of public life in the Soviet Union.

Now, they were tortured and threats were made about the safety of their families. They were accused not only of trying to murder Kirov but also of plotting with the exiled Trotsky and Nazis in Germany to kill Stalin. The trial of Zinoviev, Kamenev and 14 other Bolsheviks in August, 1936 was the most famous 'show trial'.

These show trials followed a similar pattern. The accused men appeared pale, thin and depressed in the dock. They confessed in public to a whole series of crimes they had not committed. Afterwards they were shot. News of the trials was carried in radio broadcasts, in the cinema and newspaper.

A Cartoon drawn by an opponent of Stalin and published in France in the late 1930's.

In 1937 Marshal Tukhachevsky, the Commander-in-Chief of the Red Army, was executed without trial, along with seven generals who were also said to be spies. About two thirds of all the Red Army Officers were executed or sent to labour camps. The historian Robert Conquest estimated that about eight million people were being held in these camps by 1938. Many of these prisoners had been local Communist Party leaders. Others had been lawyers, doctors, teachers, engineers, – in fact people from almost every job were 'purged'.

These first two 'show trials' were followed by a third in 1938, in which other Politburo members such as Bukharin (who had supported Stalin in the leadership struggle) and Rykov (Premier of the USSR until 1932) were purged, along with Yagoda, a former head of Stalin's Secret Police. The accusations included spying for Germany, plotting to murder Lenin and Stalin in the early 1920's and sabotaging the Russian economy. All of the accused confessed to these crimes and were executed. (They are now being re-instated in Soviet history.)

The purges continued after the Second World War. In 1945 about two million Russians who returned to their country were sent to labour camps. Stalin became more and more suspicious as he became older and his health began to fail. Even in the year of his death, 1953, he accused the doctors who were treating him of planning to

B **Life in a labour camp in the Soviet Union.**
The photograph is taken from the film 'One day in the life of Ivan Denisovich', made in Britain in the 1970's, based on Alexander Solzhenitsyn's book.

murder him. He finally died in March of that year, having murdered even more people than Hitler.

One of the ways in which we know about life during the purges is through books written by people who were sent to the labour camps. One of those writers was Alexander Solzhenitsyn. He was arrested in 1945 for criticising Stalin. He spent the next eight years in prison camps. One of his books, 'One day in the life of Ivan Denisovich' tells the story of a prisoner. The book was made into a film (see Source **B**.) Some of his writing is included in Source **E** in the chapter on the Cult of Personality. Eventually he left the Soviet Union and went to live in the USA.

C **These extracts from Solzhenitsyn's book tell us what life was like for the prisoners.**

"

Without neglecting a single fish scale or particle of flesh on the brittle skeleton, Shukhov went on champing his teeth and sucking the bones. He ate everything – the gills, the tail, the eyes when they were still in their sockets, but not when they'd been boiled out and floated in the bowl separately. Not then. The others laughed at him for that.

The cold stung. A murky fog wrapped itself around them and made them cough. The temperature out there was – 27°. The prisoners, now clad in all their rags, a cord around their wrists, their faces bound from chin to eyes with bits of cloth against the cold, waiting with leaden hearts for the order, 'Out you get'.

In the huts – mattress and grubby blanket, head on pillow stuffed with shavings of wood, feet in jacket sleeve, coat on top of blanket. No one ever took off his wadded trousers at night or you'd grow numb with cold.

"

Questions

1 a What is shown in Source **A**?
  b What do you think the cartoonist is trying to say?
2 What do you think were the advantages and disadvantages to Stalin of
  a putting old Bolshevik leaders like Zinoviev and Kamenev on trial?
  b executing army leaders like Marshall Tukhachevsky?
3 Using Sources **B** and **C**, write a paragraph to describe conditions in a prison camp.

Follow-on-question

4 Which is the more reliable source of evidence about life in a prison camp, picture **B** or document **C**? Explain your answer carefully.

The policy of the Purges

Is there any way in which the terrible suffering of millions of people in the Soviet Union in the 1930's can be explained? Historians are not the only people who have asked why all those people died. Since history involves argument, controversy and debate, there will be many different explanations. When you reach your conclusion you will have to have decided what you think Stalin was really like as a person. It is difficult to be certain about anything in history, and it is particularly hard to know what Stalin's true character was. He was a secretive person who didn't like making public appearances or speeches. There is a lot of myth about Stalin that has been built up through the incredible cult of his personality. Many Soviet documents from this period have not been released in Russia, let alone in the West. Many of the people who knew Stalin are dead and although millions of words have been written about him, a large number of them may not be very reliable. Remembering what you already know about Stalin, look at this source material about him. It provides clues about why the purges took place. Remember that the documents may say different things about Stalin and that they may all be biased. Think of *what* the document is, *who* wrote it, *when* it was written and *why* it was written or made.

B **'Stalin' by Leon Trotsky, written in Mexico, 1939.**

" Undoubtedly characteristic of Stalin is personal physical cruelty, which is usually called sadism. After he had become a Soviet dignitary he would amuse himself in his country home by cutting the throats of sheep or pouring kerosene on antheaps and setting fire to them. "

C **From Alec Nove's 'Stalinism and After', 1975.**

" Critics can also seize upon the economic weakness of Stalinism. His agricultural policies were cruel and counter-productive, and collectivisation is something for any country to avoid. If the pace and strategy of economic development by his methods required the horrors of terror and Purge, then the pace and strategy were wrong. "

A A political cartoon published in Paris in the 1930's by opponents of Stalin who had left the Soviet Union.

VISITEZ L'U.R.S.S. SES PYRAMIDES!...

D From 'The War Lords' by A.J.P. Taylor, 1978.

"

A more trivial instance to his sense of humour occurred at a large party attended by a number of generals and diplomats. Stalin called out to one of his generals: 'Bulganin, let us shoot the diplomats'. This was his form of fun.

"

E From Adam B. Ulman's 'Stalin the Man and his Era', 1974.

"

But do we need any sensational revelations to understand Stalin? No, the explanation of his life is as banal as many of Stalin's own speeches: he was corrupted by absolute power. Absolute power turned a ruthless politician into a monstrous tyrant. The terror was necessary, not only to keep men obedient, but even more to make them believe. Without terror, who would have failed to notice the patent absurdity of Stalin's rule.

"

F From Svetlana Alliluyeva's 'Twenty Letters to a Friend', 1967. She was Stalin's daughter and later left the Soviet Union.

"

My father had unpleasant memories of his journey here because he couldn't stand the sight of a crowd applauding him and shouting 'Hurrah'. His face would twitch with annoyance each time it happened.

He was accustomed by this time to having the stations empty and cleared for his arrival and to the roads he travelled on being empty. He wasn't used to people shouting and hurling themselves at his car. He had forgotten that feelings of this kind could be sincere.

G 'Stalin: a political biography by Isaac Deutsher, published in 1949 when Stalin was still alive.

"

But why did Stalin need the abominable Purge? It has been suggested that he sent the men of the old guard to their death as scapegoats for his economic failures. There is a grain of truth in this, but no more. For one thing, there was a very marked improvement in the economic condition of the country in the years of the Purge. Stalin's real and much wider motive was to destroy the men who represented the potentiality of alternative government, perhaps not of one but several governments.

"

Questions

1 List the possible reasons for the Purges given in the sources.
2 Read Sources **B** and **G**. What difference do you notice in the way in which they describe Stalin?
3 Look at Source **A**. In what ways can this cartoon be useful to a historian of Stalin's Purges?
4 Read Sources **B** and **G**.

'Trotsky's view of Stalin in Source **B** is less reliable than Isaac Deutscher's opinion in Source **C** because Trotsky was biased.'
Do you agree with this statement? Explain your answer, fully referring to the sources.
5 Look at all the sources.
'Stalin was a monster.' Do these sources show this view to be true? Explain your answer fully.

Cult of personality

This chapter deals with Stalin's propaganda. It may be helpful to consider how reliable these sources are.

At the same time as millions were suffering in the purges the rest of the Soviet people were being encouraged to love and worship their leader, Stalin. Towns were named after him – like Stalinsk, Stalino and Stalingrad. Huge posters of him were put up in public places. His picture hung in most houses. Children were encouraged to love him as the 'father' of the country (as their parents had once 'loved' the Tsar) and to inform the authorities if their parents were not loyal to him. Special paintings – like that seen in A showing Stalin and the workers at a hydroelectric dam, were commissioned by the Government.

Stalin wrote a *History of the Communist Party* in 1938 which was used in schools. Children were encouraged to learn about Stalin's part in the Revolution of 1917 – as we see in Source C.

History was being rewritten. Source B describes how the new system worked.

B **Memories of a Nadezhda Mandelstam, who had been at school in the Soviet Union of the 1930's.**

"

She showed us her school textbooks where the portraits of Party leaders had thick pieces of paper pasted over them as one by one they fell into disgrace – this the children had to do on instructions from their teacher. . . . At this time the editors of encyclopaedias and reference books were sending buyers . . . lists of articles that had to be pasted over or cut out. . . . With every new arrest, people went through their books and burned the works of disgraced leaders in their stoves.

"

Questions

1 Look at Source **A**. What 'image' of himself was Stalin trying to put across. Mention as many things as you can from the picture to back up your answer.
2 Look at Source **C**. It shows Stalin's supposed meeting with Lenin in 1917.
   a Why is Stalin seen sitting next to Lenin?
   b Which groups of people are the men supposed to come from?

A **Official Soviet painting of Stalin and the workers at a newly opened hydroelectric dam in the 1930's.**

C Official painting about 1935, showing Stalin's supposed meeting with Lenin in 1917.

D Description of a district Communist party meeting in the Soviet Union in 1938, witnessed by the writer Alexander Solzhenitsyn.

" ━━━━━━━━━━━━━━━━━━━━━━━━

At the conclusion of the conference, applause for Comrade Stalin was called for. Of course, everyone stood up (just as everyone had leapt to his feet during the conference at every mention of his name). The small hall echoed with 'stormy applause, rising to an ovation'. For three minutes, four minutes, five minutes, the 'stormy applause', continued. But palms were getting sore, and raised arms were already aching. . . . However, who would dare be the *first* to stop? After all, secret policemen were standing in the hall applauding and waiting to see *who* quit first! And in that small hall, unknown to the Leader, the applause went on – six, seven, eight minutes! . . . They couldn't stop now till they collapsed with heart attacks! At the rear of the hall, which was crowded, they could of course cheat a bit, clap less frequently, less vigorously, not so eagerly – but up there, where everyone could see them?

The director of the local paper factory, an independent and strong minded man stood, aware of all the falsity and all the impossibility of the situation. He still kept on applauding! Nine minutes! Ten! In anguish he watched the secretary of the District Party Committee but the latter dared not stop. Insanity! . . . Then, after eleven minutes, the director of the paper factory assumed a businesslike expression and sat

Questions

3 a From what you know about the history of Stalin and the Russian Revolution, how reliable would you say that Source **C** is as a source of historical evidence about the Russian Revolution?

b What is important about the fact that this picture was drawn in 1935?

Nadezhda Mandelstam last sentence in Source **B** helps us understand the two remarkable photographs shown in Sources **E** and **F** on the next page.

The first photograph shows Lenin speaking at Theatre Square, Moscow, 5 May 1920. The second picture, taken seconds later shows one very important difference and was used in 'official' history books.

Stalin was called 'the greatest genius in history and shining sun of the human race' in the official books and newspapers. Soviet writers described the way people reacted to the 'cult' of Stalin's personality at the time of the purges.

down in his seat. And, oh, a miracle took place! . . . To a man, everyone else stopped dead and sat down. They had been saved! . . .

That, however, was how they discovered who the independent people were. And that was how they went about eliminating them. That same night the factory director was arrested. They easily pasted ten years [in a labour camp] on him on the excuse of something quite different.

"

E Lenin speaking at Theatre Square, Moscow, 5 May 1920.

F Lenin speaking at the same meeting, taken about ten seconds after Source **E** and used in 'official' Soviet history books when Stalin was in power.

Questions

4 Look at Sources **E** and **F**. They show an important difference.
   a What seems to have happened in Source **F**?
   b When and why do you think this was done?
   c If Picture **F** has been 'altered', does that mean that it is of no use to a historian as a source of evidence? Explain your answer.

5 Look at Sources **D** and **F**.
   'The photograph in Source **F** is less reliable than the memories of Alexander Solzehenitsyn in Source **D** because the photograph has been tampered with.' Do you agree with this statement? Explain your answer fully, referring to the sources.

6 Look at all the sources.
   'Stalin was loved by his people.' Do these sources show this view to be true? Explain your answer fully.

Soviet foreign policy

As you read through the information and sources in this chapter about Soviet foreign policy in the 1920's and 1930's, try to work out:
- how Soviet foreign policy changed during this period, and why it changed.

In 1919 Lenin had set up an organisation called the Communist International (Comintern). Its aim was to set up Communist parties throughout the world to spread revolution. The cover of the first English edition can be seen in source **A**.

By the end of the Civil War in 1922, the Soviet economy was exhausted. It is not surprising, as within the space of nine years the USSR had been through a World War, two Revolutions and a Civil War. Lenin realised that he had to build up the strength of the Soviet Union to protect the Revolution, so he made foreign policy of secondary importance, except where it would help the economy. For example, the Treaty of Rapallo, signed in 1922, which established trading links with Germany.

Stalin continued with this policy, concentrating on 'Socialism in One Country' (see page 36). He continued to pay only lip-service to World Revolution, so his foreign policy was defensive rather than aggressive.

During the 1930's, however, Stalin had to rethink his previous ideas because of the spread of Fascism, particularly in Germany. In 1934 the USSR was accepted as a member of the League of Nations (the predecessor of the United Nations), and Litvinov, the Soviet foreign minister, looked to form alliances with other nations for defensive purposes. Stalin was desperate to avoid an attack on the Soviet Union, and in 1935 he signed a Mutual Assistance Pact with France and Czechoslovakia. The Anti-Comintern Pact was signed in 1936 by Germany and Japan (Italy joined in 1937), and Stalin now feared an attack on two fronts. Litvinov started negotiations with western powers, particularly Britain, to try to find an ally against the threat of Fascist aggression.

The Spanish Civil War broke out in 1936 (and lasted until 1939). Germany and Mussolini's Italy supported Franco, and the USSR gave aid to the other side, the Republicans. Britain and France refused to get involved, and further convinced Stalin that they were prepared to stand back and allow Fascism to wipe out Communism. This was confirmed in Stalin's mind when, at Munich in 1938, Britain and France agreed to give a part of

A Front page from the first English copy of the 'Communist International' magazine, 1919.

Czechoslovakia, the Sudetenland, to Hitler, without consulting Czechoslovakia or the USSR.

Stalin gave up trying to make an alliance with Britain and France, and astounded the world by signing the Nazi-Soviet Pact with Germany in 1939. This agreement was, basically, a non-aggression pact, but it had a secret clause which said that if Germany took west Poland, they would not object if the USSR took east Poland. Looking back, it seems that Stalin signed this Pact because he wanted to buy time before the Germans eventually invaded the Soviet Union (as Hitler had stated in his book *Mein Kampf*), and he wanted to try to create a 'buffer zone' between Germany and the USSR. A reaction to the Nazi-Soviet Pact is shown on the next page.

WONDER HOW LONG THE HONEYMOON WILL LAST?

B Cartoon by Clifford Berryman, in 'Punch',
9 October 1939.

Questions

1 Look at Source **A**.
  a What is the man doing?
  b Why is the world shown to be chained up? What do the chains mean?
  c Why is the man shown as a worker and not, for example, a banker, a factory owner or a king?
  d Does Source **A** help explain why many people in America and Western Europe in the 1920's and 1930's were very worried about the Soviet Union? Explain your answer.

2 Put these dates in a list, and write a sentence to say what happened in Soviet foreign policy against each of them: 1922, 1934, 1935, 1936, 1936–39, 1938, 1939.

3 Look at Source **B**.
  a Who is the bridegroom?
  b Who is the bride?
  c What do the signs on the wedding cake represent?
  d Why is it surprising that the bridegroom should marry this bride?
  e What does the caption 'Wonder How Long The Honeymoon Will Last?' mean?
  f Are there any clues to say which country the cartoonist came from?

Operation Barbarossa

The Nazis invaded the Soviet Union on 22 June 1941. Can you work out why?

Hitler had made it clear that he hated Communism and that it would be a fight to the death between Communism and Nazism. The uncomfortable Nazi-Soviet Pact was over. Hitler did not see any reason why his 'Blitzkrieg' tactics would not work against the Soviet Union. After all, the Nazi war machine had already beaten large parts of Europe. The Soviet army was thought to be weak and old fashioned. News of Stalin's purges (page 48) had spread all over the world. Russian armies had been defeated by Germany in the First World War. Soviet aircraft were believed to be out of date and short of spare parts.

A **Hitler gave his own reasons, to an audience of generals, in April 1941, three months before he launched the attack:**

> The Communists never have been and never will be our friends. The fight which is about to begin is a war of extermination. If Germany does not embark upon it in this spirit she may well defeat the enemy but in thirty years from now they will once again rise up and confront her.

Things went very badly for Stalin in the early part of the War. He had received many warnings that the Germans were going to attack but doesn't seem to have taken them very seriously. The Nazis conquered huge areas of Soviet land very quickly. Stalin ordered his people to destroy bridges, roads, crops – in fact anything which the Nazis could use. Villagers and factory workers were moved eastwards to areas far away from the fighting This was known as the 'scorched earth' plan. However it didn't stop the Nazis from reaching the outskirts of Moscow and surrounding Leningrad. The siege of Leningrad was to last for three years.

Three mighty Nazi armies drove the Soviet forces back (see map **B**). There was terrible loss of life. Hitler told his troops not to treat the Soviet troops and civilians according to the rules of war. Millions of Soviet people were murdered by SS (Schutz Staffel, protection squad) troops who followed behind the conquering Nazi army. Each side fought in a very brutal way. In the cold winter of 1941 the war became even tougher. Engine fuel froze in the tanks, soldiers got frostbite and supplies of weapons and clothing ran out. The Nazi armies were running out of men and beginning to lose the battle against the Russian winter.

B **Map of Operation Barbarossa.**

C **The Nazi attitude to the Slavs** from a speech by Himmler to the SS which he commanded.

"

What happens to the Russians, what happens to the Czechs, is a matter of utter indifference to me. Such good blood of our own kind as there may be among the nations we shall acquire for ourselves, if necessary by taking all the children and bringing them up among us. Whether the other peoples live in comfort or perish of hunger interests me only in so far as we need them as slaves for our culture . . . Whether or not 10,000 Russian women collapse from exhaustion while digging a tank ditch interests me only in so far as the tank ditch is completed for Germany. We shall never be rough or heartless where it is not necessary; that is clear. We Germans, who are the only people in the world who have a decent attitude to animals, will also adopt a decent attitude to these human animals, but it is a crime against our own blood to worry about them . . .

"

D **Nazi invasion of a Russian town burnt down by the departing citizens.**

Questions

1 According to Source **A**, why did Hitler invade the Soviet Union?
2 Look at Map **B**. Was the job of invading the Soviet Union a difficult one? Explain your answer.
3 **a** What was the 'scorched earth' plan?
  b Many Soviet peasants loved their land and their homes, so why do you think they destroyed them at the start of the war?
4 The Nazis murdered, shot, executed and gassed millions of people in Eastern Europe during World War Two.
  What clues can you find in Sources **A** and **C** to explain why they did this?

Follow-on questions

5 Look back at page 53.
  a What was the Nazi Soviet Pact?
  b Why might Stalin be surprised if the Germans invaded the Soviet Union?
6 Go to a library and try and find out:
  a about 'Blitzkrieg'
  b why Hitler called the attack on Russia 'Operation Barbarossa'?

Stalingrad

Stalingrad has been described as one of the most important battles of the war. See if you can find clues as to why this is so.

In April 1942 Hitler ordered his troops to smash what was left of the Soviet armies. This was no easy job. We saw in the previous chapter that the Soviet armies had recovered from the beating they took at the start of the war and, with the help of the cold winter, had halted the Nazi Blitzkrieg. They had started to attack the Nazi troops. Hitler would not think of taking a step backwards. He insisted that his troops go forward – whatever the cost. He sacked generals who dared to doubt his bold plans and ordered his armies to concentrate on destroying the Soviet economy.

He thought that the town of Stalingrad held the key to beating the Communist enemy. Stalingrad was an important centre on the River Don and was the gateway to the valuable oilfields in the Caucasus mountains (see map page 55). Besides – this town was Stalin's town and had to be destroyed.

In the summer of 1942 the Nazis launched a savage attack on Stalingrad. Massive numbers of aircraft, men and weapons were hurled at Stalingrad and eventually the army of General Von Paulus occupied the city. However Stalin was determined to recapture the city. He ordered his troops to do whatever was needed to beat the enemy. Soviet forces tried to surround Stalingrad.

Von Paulus was desperate. He begged Hitler to let him retreat from the city so as to save the army to fight another day. Hitler would not listen. He had made himself Commander in Chief of the German Army and began to take more and more decisions on his own, without listening to the advice of his experienced generals. After all, he had been right in his belief that Germany could beat the French, so he believed he would be proved right in his belief that his armies would destroy the 'subhuman' Soviets.

Against this background, Stalingrad became a huge killing ground (see Source **C**). There was bitter fighting over every street and even from house to house. Massive numbers of people on both sides were killed. Tanks pounded the buildings controlled by the other side.

Hitler ordered General Von Paulus never to surrender. Troops were told to resist the Soviet army until the end, even though they were surrounded and in danger of being completely destroyed. The end came on 31 January 1943, Von Paulus disobeyed Hitler's orders and surrendered his 100,000 men. Another 150,000 German

soldiers had been killed in the city which was to be remembered as the place in which the Soviet army proved that the mighty Nazi army could be beaten.

A Stalin, report to the 17th Congress of the Communist party of the Soviet Union, 1934.

> Our foreign policy is clear. It is a policy of preserving peace and strengthening trade relations with all countries . . . But those who try to attack our country will receive a crushing repulse to teach them in future not to poke their pig snouts into our Soviet garden.

B Stalin's Order of the Day, 28th July, 1942.

> Not a single step backward . . . You have to fight to your last drop of blood to defend every position, every foot of Soviet territory.

C 'STALINGRAD' by David Fitzpatrick, an American cartoonist, published in the St Louis Post-Dispatch, USA, 25 November 1942.

D Stalin, on 26th anniversary of the October Revolution (1943).

"

All the peoples of the Soviet Union have risen as one to defend their motherland, rightly considering the present Patriotic War the common cause of all working people, irrespective of nationality or religion.

"

E From 'The Russian Version of the Second World War' edited by Graham Lyons, 1976, a collection of extracts from Soviet school history books.

"

The battle at Stalingrad was the greatest military and political event of the Second World War. This victory turned out to be the beginning of a fundamental change in the course of the war to the advantage of the USSR and her allies. From the banks of the Volga the Red Army began its advance which eventually led to the unconditional surrender of Hitler's Germany.

The scale of the German defeat at Stalingrad was unprecedented in the history of war against the USSR.

It also upset the calculations of Turkey's rulers, who although formally neutral were in fact assisting Germany and were waiting for the fall of Stalingrad to enter the war on the side of Germany.

The Russian counter-offensive, which was launched on 19 November 1942, was a strategical stroke of the greatest significance. A stroke far greater than the Russians expected. They thought they would take 90,000 prisoners; in fact, they took over a quarter of a million. The whole German front was shattered.

"

F Russian cartoon of the new 'White' army, the dead buried under the Russian snow.

Questions

1 Why did the Nazis attack Stalingrad?
2 What do the sources and the story of Stalingrad tell us about:
   a Hitler
   b Stalin
   Give reasons for your answers.
3 Why do you think the Russians won the battle of Stalingrad?
4 Read Source **E**.
   a Why was the battle of Stalingrad important?
   b Source **E** could be said to be biased. How does the author of Source **E** show his bias? Quote from Source **E**.
   c If Source **E** is biased, does that mean it is unreliable as evidence about Soviet attitudes towards the battle of Stalingrad? Explain your answer.
5 Look at Sources **C** and **F**.
   a What do the sources show? What is happening in each cartoon?
   b What does Source **C** mean? What point do you think the cartoonist was trying to make?
   c What is the artist in Source **F** trying to say to people who look at the cartoon?
   d What do you need to know about the person who drew Source **C** to help you decide if it is reliable evidence about the battle of Stalingrad?

Looking at Eastern Europe

The next chapters deal with the Soviet Union's relations with its neighbours in Eastern Europe. It will be easier to understand the decisions Stalin and other Soviet leaders took about Eastern Europe if we look at maps of Eastern Europe. **Look at the dates on the maps and see how things changed.**

A Europe in 1914.

B Europe in 1923.

Questions

1 Look at map **A** .
  Name the four empires shown.
2 Compare map **A** and map **B**.
  a List the countries shown on map **B** which weren't there in 1914.
  b Which countries can you see on map **A** but not on map **B**?
  Which countries no longer existed in 1923?
  c Which countries appear on both maps?
  d According to map **B**, how had Germany been weakened?
  e Maps can show how boundaries changed. How big a change to the map of Eastern Europe did World War One make? Mention evidence from Maps **A** and **B** in your answer.

Follow-on questions

3 These maps can give us clues about Stalin's policies.
  Look at the following maps. Then write sentences to explain why Stalin was so keen to control Eastern Europe in 1945.
  a The map of Russia in 1914 (page 4).
  b The map of Russia in the Civil War (page 31).
  c The map of Operation Barbarossa (page 55).
  Each time explain what the map shows.

Yalta

While reading this chapter think about the condition of the USSR at this time and about Stalin's ideas of the future.

After their victory in the Battle of Stalingrad, Red Army troops continued to push the Germans back out of the Soviet Union towards Germany. Whilst they were pushing the Germans back the Red Army freed the areas which the Nazis had controlled. Stalin's critics said that one lot of invaders was simply being swapped for another.

Stalin didn't see it that way. He had plans for the future of the Soviet Union and for its relations with other countries. Those plans can only be understood if we try and find out what Stalin said in public and read what people who met him wrote about him. However there are gaps in what we know about Stalin's ideas. Perhaps we can fill in some of those gaps if we know more about the background to Stalin's decisions.

Once it became clearer that Nazi Germany was going to be beaten, the leaders of the Allies met to talk about the world which would be set up after the war. In February 1945, Stalin, Roosevelt (USA) and Churchill (UK) met at the Black Sea port of Yalta in the Soviet Union.

Stalin was well aware of the tremendous sacrifices made by the people and army of the Soviet Union in the war (Source **A**).

A 'Eyewitness' description of a journey to the Soviet Union by a foreign visitor in 1945.

"

To travel, painfully slowly, by train on the newly opened railway from Moscow to the new frontier at Brest-Litovsk in the days after the war, was a nightmare experience. For hundreds of miles, for thousands, there was not a standing or living object to be seen. Every town was flat, every city. There were no barns. There was no machinery. There were no stations, no water-towers. There was not a solitary telegraph pole left standing in all that vast landscape, and broad swathes of forest had been cut down all along the line as a protection against ambushes by partisans. All along the line lay twisted rails pulled up by the Germans who had worked with special trains fitted with great drag hooks as they moved west. In the unkempt fields, nobody but women, children, very old men could be seen – and these worked only with hand tools . . .

The houses all being gone, the people were living in dug-outs: pits dug into the earth, and roofed over with fir branches, wattle and earth – as a rule a length of stove-pipe stuck out of the humped roof scarcely lifted

above the ground. Hundreds of thousands, indeed millions, lived like this, not only all over the countryside but also amid the ruins of the great cities, Minsk, Stalingrad, Kiev. The people were not only without houses, they were dressed in rags; for four years, from 1941 until 1945, there had been no clothes of any description to be bought throughout the length and breadth of the Soviet Union. There were no boots or shoes. The peasants went about barefoot or in bast (cloth) shoes, or if they were lucky indeed, in winter the traditional felt *valenki*, worn almost to nothing. Men and women could not go to work in the factories for lack of boots and shoes; children, for the same reason, had to be kept from schools. There was very little food: the starvation years of 1941–42 were over but nearly everyone was hungry . . .

The whole country, apart from the tremendous new war industries in the east, was derelict and at a standstill.

"

Questions

1 Read Source A.
   a List the problems the Soviet Union faced at the end of the war.
   b Why do you think only 'women, children, very old men' could be seen?
2 Look at Source B. Then copy and complete the chart about Yalta (page 61). Think about why Stalin wanted the things he got at Yalta.
3 Look at Source B.
   a How was Germany made weaker?
   b How was Austria made weaker?

Follow-on questions

4 Compare Source B with Source B on page 59.
   a List the land Russia gained in 1945.
   b Does map B (on page 59) help explain why Russia took land in Eastern Europe in 1945? Explain your answer.
5 Compare all three maps of Eastern Europe. Which of these was the bigger change in the map of Eastern Europe?
   a 1914–1923
      or
   b 1923–1945
Mention evidence from all three maps in your answer.

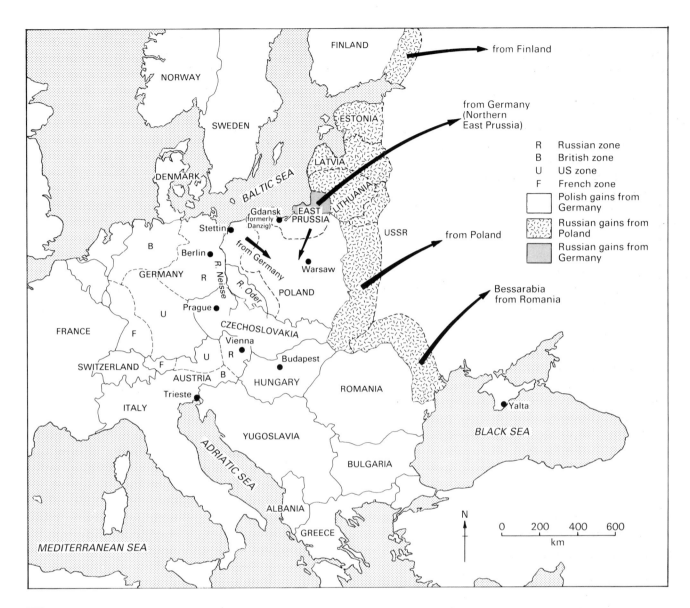

B Eastern Europe 1945

Agreed at Yalta	Why Stalin wanted this
a The Soviet Union would take land from Poland. In return Poland would get land from eastern Germany. **b** Germany would be divided up into four zones. These would be controlled by USA, France, Britain and the Soviet Union. **c** They agreed to set up a United Nations Organisation. Its aim would be to keep world peace and stop another war breaking out. The aim was to solve problems by talking and not by fighting.	

Soviet War Propaganda

This is a coursework exercise about the use of evidence. At the end of the exercise you will have to write a long paragraph to explain each of the following:

1 Why the Soviet government used propaganda during the 'Great Patriotic War' (the Second World War.) What do you think they were hoping to achieve through it?

2 Why the propaganda took the form it did. To answer this question you will need to look carefully at the different sources and to compare them. Look for things which are similar and different in the sources.

Some introductory questions have been included to help you sort out and make sense of the evidence.

Before you start remember that you will have to look at the evidence in a critical way. This means that you will have to act like any historian would when looking at sources of evidence. Think about:

  a what the evidence is
  b who made it
  c when the evidence was made
  d why the evidence was made.

The answers to these questions will help you work out how reliable the evidence is. You also need to know the context in which the evidence was made. This means that you have to understand the time or period in which the evidence was made. In this case we are dealing with the Soviet Union during the Great Patriotic War. So you will need to look back through the last few chapters. You will also need to remember what you now understand about Stalin because he was the man who controlled the propaganda. The sources will make more sense if you remember their historical background. Finally, remember that all of these sources were produced by 'official' Soviet artists working for the government as part of the war effort against Germany.

A Poster: 'Avenge the grief of the people!'

3 First we need to try and sort out these sources. Copy and complete as much of the table as you can.

	What is it?	Who made it?	When was it made?
Source **A**			
Source **B**			
Source **C**			
Source **D**			

4 a How are the Germans shown in the sources? Explain your answer carefully.
  b Why are the Germans shown in this way? Try and give reasons from what you know about the way the Soviet Union had got on with Nazi Germany before and during the Great Patriotic War.
5 a How are women shown in the sources? Explain your answer.
  b Why are women shown in this way?
6 Who do you think was supposed to see pictures like those shown in Sources **A** to **D**? What were they expected to think, feel and do when they saw them? Support your answer with the evidence from the sources.
7 a How is the Red Army shown in the sources? Explain your answer carefully.
  b Why might the Red Army be shown in this way? Suggest reasons.

Now return to write your paragraphs in response to questions 1 and 2.

C Poster: Hitler is reading news from the front of Red Army successes. 'The Red Army have trampled everything down!'

B Cartoon: 1942 repulsion of Nazi goat.

D Poster: Forward! Victory is near!

Cold War

As you read the information and look at the evidence, think about why the quarrel between the USA and the Soviet Union became so bitter.

The 'big three' (USA, USSR and Britain) met again at Potsdam in Germany in July 1945. Stalin was still leader of the Soviet Union. but Roosevelt had died and been succeeded as President of the USA by his Vice-President, Harry Truman. Churchill had lost the election of 1945 so the new British Prime Minister was Clement Attlee, the leader of the Labour Party. The war with Germany was over, but the Japanese were still fighting.

The British and Americans were angry that the Polish Communist government had moved its western border so as to take a large amount of land from Germany. Five million Germans who had been living there were said to have been expelled. The Americans said that this broke the Yalta Agreement, but the Soviet Union denied this.

Churchill was told by Truman that the Americans were ready to drop a fantastically powerful atom bomb on Japan. The full details of the bomb were not given to Stalin. On 6 August, 1945 the Americans dropped an atom bomb on the Japanese city of Hiroshima. Three days later the Soviets joined in the war against Japan. On the same day the Americans dropped a second bomb – this time on the city of Nagasaki. The Japanese surrendered almost immediately. Over 100,000 people had been killed in the two attacks and the destruction of the cities was incredible. Stalin was angry with the Americans and ordered his scientists to develop a Soviet atom bomb. Relations between the two superpowers were getting worse all the time, and Stalin was worried that the atom bomb would give the USA a great advantage.

The Iron Curtain

Churchill was Leader of the Opposition in Britain, and unhappy that the war had left Britain almost bankrupt and exhausted, and seemed to have weakened the British Empire. To many people Churchill was the hero who had led his people to victory over the Nazis, but Stalin didn't agree. Stalin thought Churchill was just as bad as the Nazis. Soviet cartoons of this period show Churchill as a Nazi who was threatening the Soviet Union. Indeed Churchill borrowed an expression first thought to have been used by the Nazi Propaganda Minister, Dr Goebbels. The expression was the 'Iron Curtain'. Churchill went to Fulton, Missouri, USA in March 1946 and gave a speech in which he declared that an 'Iron Curtain' had descended across the continent of Europe. It was separating Europe into Communist and non-Communist camps. Churchill thought that although the 'Iron Curtain' was only an imaginary line – the danger which Communism posed to the 'free' world was very real. He called for a Western Alliance to stand up to this threat. Stalin was angry and bitter about the way in which Churchill described Soviet foreign policy.

A The destruction of Hiroshima by the atom bomb.

The Truman Doctrine

Churchill had an ally in Truman. Both men were worried about what has come to be called the 'Domino Theory' (see Source **B**). When you line up a set of dominoes they will all fall if you push the first one. Truman and Churchill feared that once one country fell to Communism, others would follow. This seemed to be happening at the end of 1947, because by then most of the states of Eastern Europe had Communist governments. Further to the south there was the possibility that Communist fighters would take control of Greece. The British had been amongst those supplying the opponents of Communism in Greece with weapons, but by 1947 the British were short of cash.

Truman made a speech in March 1947 in which he set out his ideas on foreign policy. These ideas have come to be known as the 'Truman Doctrine'. He said that the USA would 'support free peoples who are resisting armed minorities' or 'outside pressures'. This meant that cash and other support would be given to people fighting Communism.

American money helped beat the Communist fighters in Greece. It would be offered again to people in many different parts of the world. Truman saw America's job as being involved in the worldwide fight against 'the enemy'. The days of Isolationism were, for the time being, over.

B **The Domino Theory.**

COMMUNISM

Questions

1 The Soviet Union was America's ally in the war. Why do you think the Americans didn't tell Stalin all about the atom bomb?

2 The atom bomb brought the war to an end, so you might have thought Stalin would be happy about it. He wasn't happy at all. Why not?

3 Copy and complete the table about the Potsdam Agreement.

Agreed at Potsdam	Why Stalin wanted this
1 The Nazi Party was disbanded and its leaders were put on trial for war crimes. 2 Each country collected goods and equipment from its zone of Germany. The Soviet Union was allowed to take some industrial equipment from the western zones, because its zone was mainly agricultural.	

4 Read the paragraph about the Iron Curtain.
  a Who is first thought to have used this expression?
  b What did Churchill mean by an Iron Curtain?
  c Churchill had spent years fighting the Nazis. How could Stalin think Churchill was as bad as the Nazis?

5 Draw a diagram of the Domino Theory (Source **A**). Underneath it, explain what it means.

6 a What was the Truman Doctrine?
  b What did it have to do with the Domino Theory?
  c Find out what 'isolationism' means.
  d Was the Truman Doctrine an isolationist policy? Explain your answer.

7 What do you think Stalin felt about the Truman Doctrine? Why?

The Marshall Plan

In June 1947 the American Secretary of State (Foreign Minister), George Marshall, announced that the USA would offer financial support to any European country which needed it.

There were many who did.

Europe was exhausted after the war and over the next four years more than $13 billions of 'Marshall Aid' was paid out to 16 countries in western Europe and to the three western zones in Germany. The money was supposed to be used to rebuild Europe's industry, but Stalin's men were suspicious of it (Source **A**). Soviet cartoons like Source **C** give you an idea of what the Soviets felt about the Marshall Plan. Stalin turned down the American money and declared that the 'satellite' countries of eastern Europe should not accept the American offer either.

The Marshall Plan is an example of how the same event can be viewed very differently by different groups of people at the same time. American and British history books often see the Marshall Plan as a brave, generous action on the part of the Americans.

How do you think Soviet history books see the Marshall Plan?

Western Europe eventually recovered from the war, and the Marshall Plan had helped in this recovery. It also provided a market for American goods. Just as the Americans accused the Soviets of using the Red Army to take over Europe, so the Soviets wondered about American ambitions in Europe. The 'Cold War' had become well and truly frosty.

A British political cartoon from the magazine 'Punch', 1947.

B From a speech at the United Nations, September 18, 1947, by Andrei Vyshinsky, Soviet Deputy Minister for Foreign Affairs.

"

This plan is an attempt to split Europe into two camps and with the help of the United Kingdom and France, to complete the formation of a bloc of several European countries hostile to the interests of the democratic countries of eastern Europe and most particularly to the interests of the Soviet Union.

An important feature of this plan is an attempt to confront the countries of eastern Europe with a bloc of western European states including West Germany. The intention is to make use of West Germany and German heavy industry as one of the most important economic bases for American expansion in Europe, in disregard of the national interests of the countries which suffered from German aggression.

"

Questions

1 a What was the Marshall Plan? Why would it help stop Communism?
  b Why do you think the Russians were suspicious of the Marshall Plan? Source **A** may help.
  c In what way was the Marshall Plan like the Truman Doctrine?

C **Soviet political cartoon from the magazine 'Krokodil', 1948.** The caption reads 'American loans in the Marshall Plan did not create much joy amongst the capitalist countries of Europe.'

Questions

2 Look at Source **C**.
  a Who was the driver of the 'Liberty Hotel' bus on the left?
  b Which two countries had he already helped onto the bus?
  c Why do you think Stalin is seen pushing Hungary onto the other bus?
  d Look at the maps of NATO and the Warsaw Pact (page 71). Which 'bus' did Bulgaria eventually join?
  e Is the cartoonist more likely to have been a supporter of Truman or of Stalin? Explain your answer.
  f Compare Source **C** with Source **B**. In what way do they disagree about who was to blame for Europe's problems after the war?
  g Why do you think Sources **C** and **B** are so different?

3 Look at Source **C**.
  a Which country is the man in the top hat supposed to come from? How can you tell?
  b Which countries are the men kneeling down supposed to come from?
  c Why is the man in the top hat shown with a face made out of a dollar?
  d Why are the men kneeling down?
  e Does the cartoonist agree or disagree with the author of Source **A** about the Marshall Plan? Explain your answer.

4 **a** The Marshall Plan is seen very differently in American and Soviet history books. Why?
  b If it is seen so differently does that mean one 'side' is lying? Explain your answer.

Stalin's last years, 1945–1953

As you read through the information and sources in this chapter, try to decide whether or not Stalin brought benefits to his people.

Stalin's main concern during this period was to try to build on the Soviet victory over Germany in 1945. He was admired for his wartime leadership which had combined communism with patriotism. However, he did not take advantage of this in his domestic policies, and soon went back to his harsh pre-war methods. As we have seen, he even started another series of purges (see page 46).

The Soviet economy had suffered terribly during the war, and another period of reconstruction was necessary. In industry, the fourth and fifth Five Year Plans were carried out (1946–50 and 1951–55). Again, consumer goods production was not the main priority, but heavy industry was targeted to make good the war losses. The following figures show the remarkable achievements that were made:

A **Soviet industrial production in 1940, 1945 and 1951.**

	1940	1945	1951
Coal	165.9	149.3	391.0 m. tonnes
Pig Iron	14.9	8.8	33.3 m. tonnes
Electricity	48.3	43.3	170.1 thousand m. kilowatt hours

There was also an increase in armaments which, again, meant that the production of consumer goods suffered.

Development in agriculture was much slower, because it was given much lower priority. Many villages had lost most of their adult male population. This meant that progress in bringing agricultural production back to its 1939 level was slowed down. As a result, it was not until the year of Stalin's death, 1953, that most agricultural goods reached their pre-war level of production again.

Soviet foreign policy during this period was dominated by the Soviet takeover of Eastern Europe and the development of the 'Cold War' (see page 64). Stalin claimed that he was carrying on the work of Lenin when, in 1947, he set up an organisation called Cominform. The aim was to bring together the many different European Communist parties so that Soviet-style Communism was the order of the day. This meant tightening control over those 'satellite' countries in Eastern Europe by strengthening the central control of the Communist Party over all aspects of life, and by introducing Collectivisation and Industrialisation policies. In 1948, Yugoslavia objected to this control. It was expelled from Cominform but remained a Communist country.

In 1949, the Soviet Union offered economic help to the satellite countries as a sort of Marshall Plan for Eastern Europe. It was known as the Council of Mutual Economic Assistance (Comecon). Stalin's position was strengthened even further with the grim news in 1949 that the Soviet Union had at last succeeded in exploding an atomic bomb. Now the Americans' nuclear monopoly was over.

The Americans replied with the successful explosion, in November 1952, of a new and even more horrifyingly deadly weapon – the H (hydrogen) bomb. The two Superpowers had entered an 'arms race'. In 1953 the Soviets exploded their own H bomb. They had more than enough deadly weapons to blow themselves – and the rest of the world – up several times over. This chilling thought remained with the world during Stalin's last days, and after his death in March 1953.

Questions

1 Study Source **B.**
  a Who is the statue of?
  b Give two possible reasons why the statue has been drawn falling over.
  c What point is the cartoonist trying to make?
  d Write your own title for the cartoon.
2 Look back over the information on Stalin's last years.
  a Make a list of the benefits Stalin brought to the Soviet people after 1945.
  b Make a list of the disadvantages for the Soviet people of these last years of Stalin's rule.
  c From the point of view of the people of the USSR, do you think they approved of Stalin's policies during this period? Explain your answer.

B 'Punch' cartoon published in 1953.

C Stalin's body lies in state in March 1953. Khruschev, who was to succeed him, stands on the far left.

Stalin: man or monster?

Source **A** gives us an idea of what a French cartoonist thought about life under Stalin. He says "We are quite happy." What do you think he *really* means?

It is clear from the information and sources on Stalin that there were both good and bad points in Stalin's rule over the Soviet Union. Whilst Stalin was alive, Soviet historians saw only the good side and they praised him. Towards the end of the 1950's, following Khrushchev's comments (see page 80), this changed to very severe criticism. Statues of Stalin were taken down and later, in the 1980's in the Glasnost years of Gorbachev, there was public criticism of Stalin in films and newspapers and a memorial to the victims of the Purges was planned.

We have the opportunity to look back on Stalin's rule and to try to see both the advantages and disadvantages of each event, and the reasons for them, and we can draw conclusions.

We have read about the horrors of the Purges, but can also see that, even though they cannot be excused, Stalin may have been worried about the threat of a takeover by the Red Army.

The Soviet people may have suffered many hardships because of a lack of production of consumer goods, but by concentrating on heavy industry it could be claimed that Stalin laid the foundations of Soviet strength which enabled the USSR to withstand Operation Barbarossa, and to finally defeat Germany in 1945.

Some historians claim that Stalin was obsessed with the idea that the Western powers wanted to overthrow the Communist regime in the USSR, but perhaps he had good reason when we consider two factors: the Western intervention in the Russian Civil War, and the development of the 'Cold War' after 1945.

The Soviet takeover of Eastern Europe has been criticised as unjust, but perhaps Stalin was worried about a possible Western invasion, similar to the one by Germany in 1941, and was simply being defensive and not aggressive.

These are just some interpretations of the various episodes during Stalin's rule of the USSR.

A French cartoon, 1935, about life in Stalin's Russia. The placard says 'We Are Quite Happy'.

Questions

1 Look back over the chapters on Stalin (pages 36 onwards). As you do so, make a list of:
   a the events for which Stalin can be criticised.
   b the events for which he can be praised.
2 Which of your lists is longer? What conclusions can we draw from this about Stalin and his methods of governing the Soviet Union?
3 Do you think that the methods Stalin used to govern the Soviet Union can be justified by the benefits he brought to his country? Explain your answer carefully.

Follow-on question

4 It has been said that dictators can only stay in power by using terror and force. Do you agree? Give reasons for your answer.

NATO

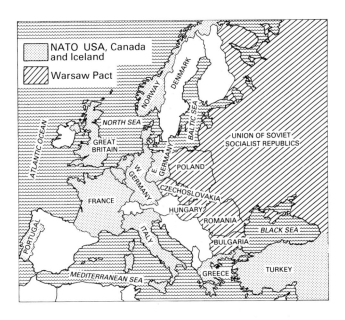

NATO (the North Atlantic Treaty Organisation) and the Warsaw Pact are military organisations to which many countries belong. NATO is led by the USA; the Warsaw Pact by the Soviet Union.

The American President Truman had felt that the Berlin Blockade was a real challenge by the Soviet Union to the West. Truman felt that force was being used to turn countries like Czechoslovakia to Communism. He wanted to do more than just rely on the United Nations to keep the peace. NATO was set up in April 1949. The countries which joined it are seen in Source **A**. Six years later the Soviet Union set up its own grouping of countries, called the Warsaw Pact (also shown in Source **A**).

A **NATO and Warsaw Pact countries.**

NATO
When NATO was set up, the Americans described it as a peaceful, defensive organisation. From what you know about the Soviet Union and the beginnings of the Cold War, try and imagine what Stalin would have thought about NATO.
For the first time in peacetime the Americans had joined a military alliance outside the American continent. American troops, planes, ships and military equipment were brought to Europe as part of the new NATO forces. Western European governments contributed as well. A NATO army of 100 divisions was planned, but the number did not rise above 30.

Questions

1 Copy and complete this chart to explain what Stalin might think the aims of NATO were.

The aims of NATO (according to the Americans)	The aims of NATO (according to Stalin)
1 To protect democracy in the North Atlantic area.	
2 NATO was linked with SEATO (South East Asia Treaty Organisation) and CENTO (Central Treaty Organisation). These had the common aim of containing Communism – all dependent on American backing.	
3 To encourage economic co-operation among members.	
4 To settle international disputes peacefully, if possible.	
5 To build up the defence systems of member countries (use of "sword and shield" policy).	
6 If one or more members were attacked it was to be considered an attack against the whole Organisation. NATO would then exercise the right to act individually or collectively in self-defence.	

The Warsaw Pact

In 1954 West Germany joined NATO. Soviet leaders were angry about this, and about the fact that West Germany had an army. The Soviet people remembered the German invasion of the Soviet Union in 1941. Now the Soviet Union seemed to be surrounded by hostile alliances.

Between 1952 and 1954 the Americans made agreements with Japan, Korea, Formosa and Spain. In that same year SEATO (South East Asia Treaty Organisation) was set up. Its members were France, Australia, Philippines, New Zealand and Thailand. The Soviet leaders saw it as another group of hostile, Communist-hating countries.

When in 1955 the Warsaw Pact was set up the Soviet leaders described it as a group of peaceful, friendly countries.

From what you know about the part Americans had played in the Cold War, try and imagine what the American President Eisenhower thought about the setting up of the Warsaw Pact. Remember that there is more information about Eisenhower, if you need it, on page 73.

Questions

2 a On an outline map of the world, use Source **A** to help you find the NATO countries. Shade them in blue.
  b Shade the Warsaw Pact countries in red.
3 a How does the chart you have completed on NATO help you understand why the Warsaw Pact was set up?
  b How does the chart you have completed on the Warsaw Pact help you understand why NATO was set up?
4 Look back at the map of Eastern Europe in 1945 (page 61).
  Then look at the map of Operation Barbarossa (page 55).
  Why was Stalin so keen to have a 'buffer zone' or 'security belt' in Eastern Europe after the war?

Questions

1 Copy and complete this chart to explain what American President Eisenhower might think the aims of the Warsaw Pact were.

The aims of the Warsaw Pact (according to the American President Eisenhower)	The aims of the Warsaw Pact (according to the Soviet Union)
1 A treaty of friendship, co-operation and mutual assistance.	
2 Wherever possible, international disputes involving members were to be settled peacefully.	
3 To work towards a general reduction in arms.	
4 In the event of an armed attack upon a member country the Pact would exercise the right, as stated in the UN Charter, to act individually or collectively in self-defence.	

The Thaw 1953–1961

The title of this suggests that there was an improvement in Superpower relations. **As you look at the information try and work out how big that improvement was.**

Stalin died in 1953, but many of his policies and ideas lived on. The Cold War did not suddenly end with Stalin's death, but some of its tensions died with him. By 1953 both the Soviet Union and the Americans had the H (hydrogen) bomb, so there was always the danger lurking beneath the surface that any war between these Superpowers could bring about the end of the world. Maybe this deadly thought helped bring about a new approach to relations between the two countries.

It was Khrushchev who emerged as the successor to Stalin (see page 78), and he brought with him a new style of leadership. In a speech at the Twentieth Communist Party Congress in February, 1956, he not only criticised Stalin's domestic policies, but put forward the idea that the Soviet Union and the Americans had to learn to live together peacefully in the nuclear age. He said, 'There are only two ways – either peaceful co-existence or the most destructive war in history.'

This did not mean that Khrushchev no longer wanted a Communist world, but it did mean that peace was vital. He explained that 'we communists believe that the idea of communism will be victorious throughout the world. Many will probably disagree with us. It is their right to think so. We may argue, we may disagree with each other. The main thing is to keep to arguing without resorting to arms in order to prove that one is right.'

The Americans did not stop being suspicious of the Soviet Union when Stalin died. Indeed, have they stopped being suspicious of the Soviet Union today? Dwight Eisenhower had become President of the USA in 1952. He had been Supreme Allied Commander in World War Two, and after the war was made the first Commander in Chief of NATO. He hated Communism, and his Secretary of State (foreign minister), John Foster Dulles, had similar views. Dulles said, 'We shall never have a secure peace or a happy world so long as Soviet Communism dominates one third of all the peoples that there are, and is trying to extend its rule to many others.' Dulles wanted to 'free' those people he thought were imprisoned by Communism. The terror continued.

The Soviets were worried about the setting up of NATO and SEATO (see page 71), and the Americans were worried about the formation of the Warsaw Pact and the crushing of the Hungarian Uprising (see page 75). Dulles threatened that if the USSR attacked the USA, then the USA would strike back with a 'massive retaliation' of H-bombs. This dangerous gamble showed that Dulles was prepared to go right to the very edge – or to the brink – to get what he wanted. This policy was called 'Brinkmanship'.

On 4 October, 1957, the Soviet Union launched the Sputnik. It was the first satellite ever put into space. The rocket which launched it was, of course, capable of carrying a nuclear bomb to destroy a city in the USA.

So with all these dangerous things happening, you might be forgiven for wondering if relations between the Soviet Union and the USA could get much worse. In fact, Khrushchev made efforts to improve understanding between East and West when he made a visit to London in 1959 to talk to Prime Minister Macmillan. That same year, Khrushchev went to the USA and held discussions with President Eisenhower. Plans were made for another meeting between the two men in May 1960 in Paris.

Then an event took place which helped bring about an end to the 'thaw' in the Cold War. Just before the Paris meeting was going to take place, an American U2 spy plane was shot down over the Soviet Union. Its pilot, Gary Powers, was put on trial. Khrushchev made the most of the incident, and claimed that it showed the world what the Americans were really up to. Eisenhower refused to apologise to Khrushchev. The Paris meeting was over before it had taken place.

On 12 August, 1961, East German workers began building a wall to separate East Berlin from West Berlin. Ever since the end of the war there had been tension between East and West about Berlin. The USA and the Soviet Union had come close to war during the Berlin Blockade crisis (see page 71). Tension had increased in the 1950's when West Germany joined NATO. Now the Soviets explained that a 'freedom wall' was needed to keep capitalist spies out of East Berlin. Newspapers in the West claimed that the wall was built to stop East Berliners from 'escaping to the free world'. Opponents of the wall said that thousands of East Berliners wanted to get away from the low wages, poor housing and lack of freedom in the Communist world. Now there was a barrier of bricks, stones and minefields, as well as the barrier of fear, mistrust, ignorance and suspicion which separated the two sides.

A Cartoon by 'Vicky'. It appeared in the British publication 'New Statesman' on 14 May, 1960.

Questions

1 Put these dates in the margin, and write a sentence to say what happened in East-West relations against each of them: 1953, 1956, October 1957, 1959, May 1960, August 1961.

2 Look at Source **A**.

  a What type of plane is shown in the cartoon?

b Why is it shown hitting the dove?

c Why is Khrushchev seen on the other side of the mountain from Macmillan, Eisenhower and De Gaulle?

d What do you need to know about the author of the cartoon so as to find out if it is reliable as evidence about this incident?

Hungarian and Czech crises

Relations between the Soviet Union and its neighbours in Eastern Europe have not always been easy. Read these stories of two problems and see if you can find ways in which they are similar or different. Then copy and complete the chart on page 77.

Hungary

The Red Army helped free Hungary from Nazi control in 1945. They brought Communist ideas with them. In November 1945 elections were held and the Communists got less than 20% of the vote. However the Communists managed to take over most of the important jobs in the Government. The Communist leader Matyas Rakosi used the words 'salami tactics' to describe the way in which his opponents were gradually sliced away like pieces of a sausage. He used the Secret Police to arrest opponents. He won the election of 1947. He said that this proved that the people of Hungary wanted a Communist Government. His opponents said that he cheated in the election and used his victory as an excuse to get rid of opposition political parties and control the newspapers. Some of the Government's opponents were put on trial.

Rakosi introduced Stalinist policies like Collectivisation and Industrialisation. Hungary joined the Communist Economic System in Eastern Europe. Critics of the system said that Collectivisation wasn't working well, and that the Soviet Union did better than Hungary in trade between the two countries.

After Stalin's death in 1953 the Stalinist policies were relaxed a little and a new Communist leader called Imre Nagy took over the Government. He began to introduce new policies. Many political prisoners were freed. Students and workers demonstrated in the streets to show their support for Nagy's government. Then in 1955 Rakosi and his supporters forced Nagy to leave the Government. It looked as if all the old Stalinist ideas were going to come back. When Khrushchev dared to criticise Stalin in a speech in 1956, people in Hungary continued their criticisms of Rakosi's government. Huge crowds came out into the streets of the Hungarian capital Budapest and called for Rakosi to resign and Nagy to come back.

In October 1956 their wishes were granted. Nagy agreed to allow elections in which other political parties could take part – not just the Communist Party. Soldiers, workers, peasants and students supported the new Government. In November Nagy announced that Hungary would withdraw from the Warsaw Pact. This was too much for the Soviet Union. Hungary was invaded by Soviet troops and tanks. There was fighting in the streets of Budapest and it is thought that about 3000 people died and 200,000 Hungarians fled to the West. Nagy was arrested and executed.

A new government, led by Janos Kadar, took over. It was prepared to stay in the Warsaw Pact and to co-operate with the wishes of the Soviet Union.

Czechoslovakia 1968

One of the most dramatic events in Soviet relations with east European countries took place in 1968. Soviet tanks were sent into Czechoslovakia.

As you read the evidence think about why the Soviet tanks were sent in and what this tells us about Soviet relations with its neighbours. The Red Army had helped free Czechoslovakia from Nazi control in 1945. In the elections of 1946 the Communists were the most popular party. Communists were powerful in the police and the army.

Czechoslovakia had 'gone communist' in 1948. Klement Gottwald carried out Stalinist policies, introducing Collectivisation and Industrialisation. There were 'show trials' like those in the Soviet Union of the 1930's.

Gottwald died of a chill he caught at Stalin's funeral in 1953 and was replaced as leader by Antonin Novotny. He continued the Stalinist policies. His critics claimed that he didn't invest enough money in new farm machinery for the Collectivisation programme. They also said that the trade balance between the Soviet Union and its 'satellites' was unfair, in that the Soviets were taking about 40% of Czechoslovakia's foreign trade by the 1960's. The press was censored and there were controls on the freedom of speech.

Eventually in January 1968 Novotny's critics in the leadership of the Communist party forced him to quit. The leading figure in the new government was Alexander Dubcek, the First Secretary of the Party. He gained the support of President Svoboda and Prime Minister Cernik for a new set of government policies. These were introduced in the spring of 1968, the so-called 'Prague spring'.

Dubcek's Policies

1   The Communist Party would not interfere so much in the running of the country. Workers would have more say in the running of factories.
2   'Socialism with a human face' would be introduced. This would allow for freedom of speech, a free press and more choice in the running of the country.
3   There was talk about freedom for political parties which did not agree with the Communist Party.

Dubcek said that Czechoslovakia would still be a Communist country and a member of the Warsaw Pact. He hoped that the Soviet Union would allow Czechoslovakia to find its own way to Communism.

Not everyone agreed with him. Newspapers in East Germany criticised Dubcek. They said that 'servants of imperialism' and 'enemies of the people' were running the country. On the other hand, newspapers in countries like the USA and Britain praised Dubcek's policies. Students and workers held demonstrations to show their support for the new policies.

The Soviet leader Leonid Brezhnev (who had taken over in 1964) warned Dubcek that they should not go too far. On 21 August tanks from the Soviet Union and other Warsaw Pact countries invaded Czechoslovakia. The Czech people came out into the streets and talked to the troops, but they did not fight. Within a year Dubcek had been dismissed from his job, along with most of his supporters. Gustav Husak took over the leadership and did as much as possible to return to the situation before Dubcek's 'Prague spring'. Czech newspapers declared that the Soviet tanks had protected 'freedom and socialism' in Czechoslovakia. Dubcek's policies were abandoned.

Questions

1 a   Copy the three points from the box titled *Dubcek's Policies*.
  b   Suggest reasons why the Soviet government might have been worried by these policies.
2   Briefly describe the part played by each of these men in the Czechoslovakia story: Klement Gottwald, Antonin Novotny, Alexander Dubcek, Leonid Brezhnev.
3   Look at Source **B**.
  a   Which country does the soldier come from? How can you tell?
  b   Why has the cartoonist included the date 1945 in the left hand box?
4   Look at Source **A**.
  a   Name three clues to do with the Nazis in the cartoon.
  b   To whom does the big hand belong? What is it doing?
  c   What point do you think the person who drew Source **A** was trying to make about the invasion of Czechoslovakia by Warsaw Pact troops?

A **Cartoon from the newspaper 'Izvestia' 22 August 1968, the day of the occupation of Prague by Warsaw Pact troops**. The armband says "Imperialism" and the word at the bottom is "Czechoslovakia"

B Cartoon, 1968

Question

5 The two cartoons give very different ideas on what the occupation of Czechoslovakia was all about. Does that mean one of the two cartoonists was lying? Explain your answer.

Further Questions

1 Copy and complete the chart.

	Questions	Hungary 1956	Czechoslovakia 1968
a	What did the Red Army do in 1945?		
b	How did the Communists do in the elections just after the Second World War?		
c	What else did the Communists do to get to power?		
d	What socialist policies did the Government bring in when it got to power?		
e	Why were some people unhappy with the Communist Government? List reasons.		
f	Why was the Soviet Government worried about what was happening?		
g	Who led the protests? What was his job?		
h	What happened to the leader of the Uprising after the Soviets had taken control?		
i	What type of Government took over once the Soviets took control? What did it do?		

2 Look at your answers to the chart. Do you think the Hungarian and Czech problems were very similar, or were they different? Explain your answers.

3 a Read about the Solidarity crisis in Poland in 1980 (page 80) and fill out another column for the chart. Give it the title 'Solidarity' 1980.
   b Was the Solidarity crisis more like the Hungarian crisis or the Czech Crisis? Explain your answer.

Khrushchev, 1953–1964

As you read through this chapter, try to work out how and why Khrushchev changed Stalin's domestic policies.

After the death of Stalin, it was not clear who would succeed him. We have seen how Stalin feared anyone in his Politburo who became too powerful, and so no-one was in a position to take over automatically. It was felt that one person should not hold such absolute power again, so rule was shared between Malenkov, who became Prime Minister, and Nikita Khrushchev, the Party Secretary. By 1955, however, Khrushchev had emerged as sole leader. He was the son of a peasant and, although he did not have the manner of a leader, he must have been intelligent to have survived under Stalin.

He set out on a policy of 'De-Stalinisation', which meant undoing many of the hated policies of his predecessor. This began at the Twentieth Communist Party Congress in 1956 when Khrushchev criticised 'the man who was always right'. He said that it was wrong to turn a man into a godlike figure.

A Part of the speech given by Khrushchev at the Twentieth Communist Party Congress, 1956.

> Such a man supposedly knows everything, sees everything, thinks for everyone and is never wrong in his behaviour.

Khrushchev complained that Stalin had gone against Lenin's methods of proving to the people that the Communist system was right, and of educating them in the new ways. Instead he used methods of:

> ... violence, mass repressions and terror. Confessions of guilt were gained with the help of cruel and inhuman tortures ...

Even though most Russians knew these facts, this speech shocked many of them. However, many were pleased that the long period of fear and repression seemed to be over. Following this, statues of Stalin were pulled down, cities like Stalingrad were renamed and Stalin's place in the official history books was made more realistic.

Khrushchev wanted to rule the country in a totally different way. He wanted to be popular, more of a man of the people. Fewer people were punished for speaking out against the government, and politicians who were thrown out of the Politburo and other top positions were given lesser jobs rather than being executed.

Khrushchev wanted to improve the standard of living, and he embarked on policies which were called 'goulash communism' (a mixture of different ideas about economic policy). He abandoned the current Five Year Plan in favour of another which placed more emphasis on producing consumer goods. He met with some opposition from within the Party and the Army on this, but he managed to improve the standard of living considerably. Bonus systems were introduced to persuade workers to produce more.

Khrushchev met with less success in his agricultural policies. He used two new methods: the introduction of 'incentives' by which peasants were paid a proportion of their Collective's profits, and the Virgin Lands Scheme which aimed to plough up and use uncultivated land in Siberia. In the short term there were dramatic improvements. Grain production rose from 83m. tons in 1953 to 140m. tons in 1962. But no account had been taken of the fact that the quality of soil was poor. Gradually, the land was worn out, and in 1963 the production figure for grain was down to 110m. tons, and down again the next year, as shown in the following table:

B A summary of economic production figures under Khrushchev.

	1954	1964
Steel	42m. tonnes	85m. tonnes
Crude Oil	59m. tonnes	224m. tonnes
Cloth	159000 tonnes	239000 tonnes
Wheat	42m. tonnes	74m. tonnes
Cattle	57m.	85m.
Radios & TVs	3,154,000	4,766,000
Cars	95,000	185,000

Khrushchev's very individual policies at home were becoming unpopular and unsuccessful. He was ousted from power in 1964 whilst on a holiday by the Black Sea. However, it was probably the failure of his foreign policy which was the main reason for his downfall.

C **The different rates of growth in the economies of the USSR, France, England and USA**, as shown in a Soviet school textbook published while Khrushchev was leader of the Soviet Union.

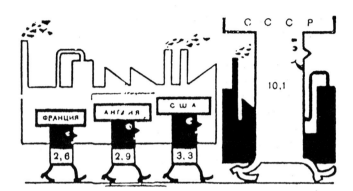

D **The different rates of growth in the economies of certain countries between 1950–1964**, published in an English school textbook.

Comparative growth rates of gross national product

(Annual averages)

Country	Aggregate		Per capita	
	1950–58	1958–64	1950–58	1958–64
USSR	7·1	5·3	5·2	3·5
France	4·4	5·4	3·5	4·0
West Germany	7·6	5·8	6·4	4·6
Italy	5·6	6·1	5·0	5·4
United Kingdom	2·4	3·9	1·9	3·1
Japan	6·1	12·0	4·8	11·0
United States	2·9	4·4	1·2	2·7

Questions

1 Study Source **B**.
  a Which of the products mentioned in the table are consumer goods?
  b Describe what happened to the production of consumer goods between 1954–64.
  c From your answers to **b**, do you think Khrushchev did enough for the living standards of the people of the Soviet Union during this 10 year period? Explain your answer.
2 According to Source **C**, which country had the highest rate of growth?

3 Compare Source **C** with Source **D**.
  a What difference do you notice in the rates of growth shown in these two sources?
  b Why do you think the sources give such different figures?
4 'Sources C and D prove that you can't trust figures as evidence about the Soviet economy under Khrushchev.' Do you agree? Explain your answer.

Follow-on question

5 Who did most for the living standards of the average Soviet citizen, Stalin or Khrushchev? Give evidence to support your answer.

The Brezhnev years

Leonid Brezhnev (1906–1982)

Brezhnev was born in the Ukraine, the son of an industrial worker. He joined the Communist Youth Organisation (Komosomol) and, in 1931, became a full member of the Communist Party. He qualified as an engineer. A loyal follower of Stalin, he was rewarded in 1939 by promotion in the local Party.

During the 'Great Patriotic War' he helped Krushchev in the fight against the Nazis on the Southern Front. After the war he was given the job of rebuilding his homeland, the Ukraine. Brezhnev's promotion in the Party continued. In 1952 he was elected to the Central Committee. When Krushchev fell from power in 1964, it is said that Brezhnev's plotting pushed him. In 1966 he took the title of Secretary-General of the Communist Party and was clearly in charge until his death in office at the age of 75.

He was followed as Soviet leader by Andropov and Chernenko, neither of whom survived long at the top, thus making way for the new, much younger, leader Mikhail Gorbachev in 1985.

A **In 1979 President of the Presidium of the USSR Supreme Soviet Leonid Brezhnev at an international children's festival.**

Leonid Brezhnev was the leading politican in the Soviet Union in the 18 years following the fall from power of Nikita Khrushchev in 1964. Sources **A**, **B** and **C** show stages in Brezhnev's life. As you read about his career see if the events of that career match up with the 'image' given in the paintings.

During Brezhnev's period in power the Soviet Union adopted the policy of 'detente'. There were problems with the Soviet Union's neighbours in eastern Europe. In 1968 Soviet tanks occupied Czechoslovakia (page 77).

Brezhnev and Solidarity 1980

Brezhnev was faced with a crisis in Poland in 1980 when a trade union leader called Lech Walesa became rather more influential and important than the Soviet government might have liked.

The roots of the problem were centuries old. The Poles had often suffered from being 'sandwiched' in between two more powerful countries, Russia and Germany. The Polish people suffered terrible loss of life in World War Two and saw themselves the victims of the Nazi-Soviet Pact (see page 56). The Red Army 'liberated' Poland at the end of the war, but many Poles suspected that the Russians were responsible for many atrocities in Poland.

The Red Army brought a Communist Government to Poland and helped make sure that the western backed government in exile during the war did not return to power. The Communists won the elections, but their opponents accused them of cheating, and of arresting opposition politicians. Collectivisation and Industrialisation were introduced and Poland joined the Soviet economic, military and political groupings. However, the Catholic Church remained powerful in Poland and had millions of followers. It stood for a set of ideas which were the opposite of the State sytem.

The Government had problems in convincing the farmers that Collectivisation was good for them, and in persuading Poles that the economic system was working. There were regular shortages of food and consumer goods in the shops, and when the Government put prices up there was trouble on the streets and in the factories. In 1956 there were strikes about wages and conditions by engineering workers in the industrial town of Poznan. These led to demands for political change which the Government had to respond to.

However, the same complaints were heard again in 1970 when shipyard workers in Gdansk went on strike. Some of them were killed by Government troops. Gomulka was replaced as First Secretary by Edward Gierek. He made promises to modernise the economy, but the basic problems remained. Poland owed huge debts to the West. By 1981 more than 75% of Poland's export trade went on paying the interest on past debts. Wages rose, but food prices were kept artificially low because the Government feared riots if prices went up.

In 1980, an electrician called Lech Walesa led a strike in the Lenin Shipyard in Gdansk. He wanted better wages and working conditions and recognition for his Solidarity Trade Union. The 1970 story was repeated. Demands for pay and conditions soon turned into more general demands: for a free press, more democracy, free trade unions, etc. This time the unrest spread all over the country. There was even a 'Rural Solidarity' Union set up amongst the farm workers. The government fell and there was talk of Solidarity being a 'total social movement'. This alarmed Brezhnev, and the Soviet leaders considered using force to break Solidarity. In the end, no Soviet tanks were used. However, the military government imposed martial law in December 1981. Lech Walesa was imprisoned for a time. Solidarity was banned. The Soviet system had been restored.

There are questions about the Solidarity episode in the chapter about uprisings in Hungary and Czechoslovakia (see page 75).

Brezhnev was still in control of Soviet policy when in 1980 Soviet troops occupied Afghanistan. Brezhnev had shown great skill in winning power from Khrushchev and then holding onto power for so long. Large amounts of money were put into military spending and the control of the Communist Party over all aspects of Soviet life was strengthened. However when Brezhnev died in 1982 the country was still waiting for major economic changes. These were to be attempted when Mikhail Gorbachev came to power in 1985.

Questions

1 Put each of these dates on a separate line in the margin. Next to each date say what happened to Leonid Brezhnev: 1906, 1923, 1931, 1939, 1952, 1964, 1966, 1980, 1982.

2 The photograph of Leonid Brezhnev (Source **A**) show him with a group of children from many countries.

   a Why do you think Brezhnev (and other leaders) have their photographs taken with children?

   b Why do you think that showing the leader with children of different nationalities has special advantages?

   c What is the purpose of such photographs?

Further Question

3 In recent years Brezhnev's period as leader has been criticised within the Soviet Union. What examples of this type of criticism of the past Soviet leadership, coming from Soviet sources, can you find from newspapers and on television.

The Arms Race

Diagram **A** shows events from the nuclear arms race. The Soviet Union has played an important part in this arms race, but it is the Americans who could be said to have started it because it was they who bombed Hiroshima in 1945.

As you look at the information and the sources, think about what an arms race is and what it means for the governments involved in it.

The Threat of Nuclear War
By 1949 Stalin's scientists had tested their own atom bomb. Soon both the Americans and the Soviets had even more powerful bombs. The dangers were enormous.

During the Korean War (1952–3 in which the East supported the Communist North, and the West supported the South) the American military commander, MacArthur, had put forward the idea that a nuclear bomb be used to end the war. Similar ideas were to be advanced by other people in a later war – in Vietnam.

Each time the American President stood back from the brink of nuclear war, but as we saw in the chapter on the 'thaw' (page 73) the actual idea of going to the brink of nuclear war had been put forward by an American Secretary of State called John Foster Dulles.

The Soviet leader Khrushchev announced that he believed in 'peaceful coexistence' with the West. However he also knew that it could benefit the Soviet Union if he could take the lead in the 'space race'. This happened in 1957 when a Soviet Inter-Continental Ballistic Missile was launched. In 1962 the Soviets sent ICBMs to Cuba. This led to the Cuban Missile Crisis of that year, but the missiles were withdrawn.

In the same year the Soviet Union announced the successful launch of the Sputnik satellite. The Americans did their best to reply and by the early 1960's each side had put astronauts into space.

The race for the Moon and the building of space stations and reusable spacecraft caught the imagination of the public. However it should not be forgotten that each side saw the military uses to which satellite technology could be used.

The figures published by the Americans show that far more military satellites than 'scientific' satellites were launched. The Soviet Union did not publish its results in the same way, but it is believed that the emphasis on military matters was the same.

In the 1980's the Soviet leaders were complaining that the Americans were extending the arms race into space, with the launch of the

US 1945	atomic bomb	1949 USSR
US 1948	intercontinental bomber	1959 USSR
US 1954	hydrogen bomb	1955 USSR
USSR 1957	intercontinental ballistic missile (ICBM)	1958 USA
USSR 1957	man-made satellite in orbit	1958 USA
US 1960	submarine-launched ballistic missile	1968 USSR
US 1966	multiple warhead (MRV)	1968 USSR
USSR 1968	anti-ballistic missile (ABM)	1972 US
US 1970	multiple independently targeted warhead (MIRV)	1975 USSR
US 1980	new long-range cruise missile	? USSR
US 1984	S.D.I.	? USSR
US 1988	Treaty to reduce intermediate nuclear weapons	1988 USSR

A Events in the Arms Race

SDI ('strategic defence initiative') research programme.

It is no coincidence that the nickname of SDI was 'star wars'. President Reagan claimed that SDI would give the USA a 'shield of peace' which would help reduce the risk of nuclear war. The Soviet leaders complained that SDI only increased the danger of disaster, and tried to link arms reductions to the ending of SDI.

So the possibility that the world could one day be destroyed in a nuclear war has remained with us since the end of the Second World War in 1946. During the Cuban Missile Crisis that possibility almost became a horrifying reality.

Perhaps it took such a terrifying crisis to force the two sides into a different relationship, and since the Cuban Missile Crisis a number of attempts have been made to stand back from the edge of nuclear disaster.

1 Nuclear Test Ban Treaty, 1963: After the Cuban Missile Crisis all forms of nuclear testing – except underground testing – were banned. Even though France and China refused to sign, the Treaty was generally welcomed.

2 'Hot Line' 1963: The American and Soviet leaders agreed that a direct telephone link between their offices be installed. The hope was that contact would be improved, particularly in times of crisis, so that another incident like the Cuban Crisis might be avoided.

3 Non-Proliferation Treaty 1968: It had become clear that each side could destroy the other. This horrifying idea came to be known as 'Mutually Assured Destruction' – or MAD. The Soviet leader Brezhnev and the American President Johnson agreed to deny nuclear technology to those smaller, emerging countries which wanted it.

4 Strategic Arms Limitation Talks (SALT) 1972: Johnson was succeeded as President by Richard Nixon. He made an agreement with Brezhnev to limit the spread of 'strategic' nuclear weapons. The problem was that each side was modernising its weapons and building different types of weapons. The SALT process was part of an increased understanding, or detente.

5 SALT 2 1979: President Carter met Brezhnev in Vienna and agreed on another treaty to try and slow down the spread of nuclear weapons. However when Ronald Reagan became President there was a change of attitude in the corridors of power. The American Senate refused to ratify (confirm) the treaty, so Carter's plans were not carried out.

6 Strategic Arms Reduction Talks (START) 1982: Ronald Reagan had described the Soviet Union as the 'evil empire'. He agreed with the policy of his Defence Secretary, Caspar Weinberger, which had been to order a massive increase in America's defence forces. The prospects of reducing nuclear weapons did not look at all good at the end of the 'summit' meeting between Reagan and Secretary General Gorbachev (who had taken over in 1985 from Chernenko) at Rekjavik in 1986. The two men had not reached an understanding at all and the row about SDI continued.

7 Washington Summit, 1987: Reagan and Gorbachev met again and this time they managed to reach agreement on reducing intermediate nuclear weapons. Both sides praised it as an historic moment.

Questions

1 Look at Source **A**.
  a What is an 'arms race'?
  b When did the nuclear arms race begin?
  c Why do you think Stalin felt he had to join the arms race?
  d Why is the arms race so expensive?
  e Look at the column for 1988 in Source **A**. In what way is it different from the other events on Source **A**?
  f Is the arms race difficult to stop? Explain your answer.
  g Can there be anything good about an arms race? Are there any benefits? Give reasons for your answer.
2 Copy Source **A** and add pictures to show any recent developments in the arms race.

Glasnost and Perestroika

The person who took over as Soviet leader in March 1985 was Mikhail Gorbachev. He soon came to be associated with two ideas — *Glasnost* (openness) and *Perestroika* (restructuring).

As you read the information and the sources of evidence, try and work out what these ideas involved. Also think about the changes which Glasnost and Perestroika brought to the Soviet system. The evidence put forward in this chapter is a series of articles from British newspapers from April and May 1988 (three years into Gorbachev's rule). Look for things which changed and things which stayed the same.

Before examining the evidence we need to know a little about the background to Glasnost.

Mikhail Gorbachev was a very different type of leader from those who had come before him (see Source **A**). He had not even been born when Lenin died and he did not owe his rise to power to Stalin. He was not afraid to go out and 'meet the people' in the type of public appearance more usually associated with western politicians and royalty, rather than reclusive, secretive Soviet leaders.

The American President Reagan was known as 'the great communicator', but Gorbachev was skilled in putting over his ideas too. He needed great skill to tackle some of the very difficult problems facing the Soviet Union.

Soviet troops had been stuck in a messy war in Afghanistan since 1980. Gorbachev had to try and find a way of getting out of the conflict which had been nicknamed the Soviet Union's 'Vietnam', because the Superpower seemed unable to win it.

He was faced with mounting economic problems. The huge amounts of money spent on the arms race meant that badly needed modernisation of the economy could not easily take place. There were still queues in the shops. From time to time there were very serious problems with the harvest, so the Soviet Union had to import grain from America. The Stalinist system of Collectivisation needed bringing up to date. Unlike all his predecessors, Gorbachev's special training was in agriculture, so he understood how great the difficulties were.

The Stalinist problems of bureaucracy and too much control from Moscow made it difficult for changes to be brought in. Gorbachev knew that it wasn't just a question of producing better consumer goods. The real problem was that Gorbachev felt that the Soviet Union needed more democracy. People needed more of a say in the running of the economy and even of the government. This was no easy idea to accept in a country in which there was only one political party, and thousands of officials who had every interest in keeping things the way they had always been.

There is an old saying: 'The most dangerous time for a government is when it starts to reform.' Mikhail Gorbachev started to reform the Soviet system, but he had some powerful opponents from the old system. He knew that by the year 2000 Muslims will make up one quarter of the population of the Soviet Union. There were riots in provinces as far apart as Latvia in the Baltic and Armenia, near Turkey. Several religious groups demanded more freedom. Opponents of the government pressed for equality and freedom. Stories about the worst parts of the old Stalinist system were heard in public.

How did Gorbachev respond to these problems?

How much change did he introduce?

How much remained the same?

C Murray's Handbook for Travellers in Russia, 1893.

> Of course nothing like liberty of the press is known in Russia. There is in fact hardly any press, in the common acceptation of the term as the only newspapers are published by the government, and no periodical literature of at all a political character exists in the Russian language. A strict censorship as to all books imported from abroad is established to prevent the introduction and diffusion among the mass of the people of any dangerous doctrines or unwelcome pieces of news . . .

Questions

1 What do 'Glasnost' and 'Perestroika' mean?
2 List the problems Gorbachev faced when he took power in 1985.

D Soviet leaders at the Lenin Mausoleum, May Day 1988.

Up-to-date

On these pages there are headlines, articles and a cartoon which appeared in British newspapers during a few months in 1988. While you have been reading this book, many other similar articles will have appeared in the newspapers; you will have seen events about the Soviet Union on the television and heard about them on the radio. History is continuing to be made.

As you read, listen and watch, think about how some things are changing in the Soviet Union and how others are staying the same.

A The Independent, 17 November, 1988.

Estonian assembly rejects Moscow's plans for reform

Dissidents use capitalist razzmatazz

By Anne Spackman

CAR STICKERS and T-shirts made in Britain are being distributed in their thousands in the Soviet Baltic states and Eastern Europe as part of a campaign to harness the youthful side of anti-Moscow feeling.

B The Independent, 19 November, 1988.

Russia to play down military element in anniversary parade

Jonathan Steele in Moscow

THE Soviet Union is planning a more modest display of its military hardware for the annual Revolution Day celebrations this year, with no new weapons on show for the first time since President Gorbachev came to power.

Gulag victims look for penal reform

By Anne McElvoy

President Gorbachov's announcement of the impending release of political prisoners will have raised the hopes of many people detained in the Soviet Union for a plethora of "crimes against the state". But few can be sure that their cases fall within the scope of his leniency.

C The Guardian, 1 November, 1988.

D The Times, 29 October, 1988.

E The Daily Telegraph, 18 November, 1988.

Soviet Union 'bigger threat than before'

By Ian Ball In New York

MR GORBACHEV, the Soviet leader, who is to meet President Reagan and President-elect Bush in less than three weeks, was the target of an unexpectedly tough speech by Mr William Webster, the CIA director.

He told the Yale Political Union at New Haven, Connecticut, on Wednesday night that the Soviet Union was a greater threat to American interests now than before Mr Gorbachev came to power.

Mr Webster said: "I believe that our relationship is likely to remain essentially adversarial," despite whatever arms control agreements the United States made with the Soviet Union.

"The Soviet Union's military capability, its efforts to increase global influence and its aggressive intelligence activities are still serious threats to United States interests."

Soviets 'in arms strategy shift'

**Hella Pick
Diplomatic Correspondent**

AFTER years of calling for nuclear disarmament, the Soviet Union is close to accepting Nato's doctrine of military stability, based on a mix of nuclear as well as conventional arms, according to Mr Manfred Woerner, Nato's Secretary General.

F The Guardian, 24 November, 1988.

Russian historian says Stalin killed at least 12 million

G The Times, 31 October, 1988.

Workers' unrest on the increase

Novosibirsk, Feb 29: Savings bank employees refused to serve customers, demanding better conditions and more workspace. Management went some way to satisfying them, and the strikers returned after a day and a half.

Tallinn, Apr 14: Lathe operators struck over failure to carry out repairs. Workers complained of union inaction.

One consequence of President Gorbachov's reform programme has been a substantial increase in worker unrest throughout the Soviet Union. Often strikes are called because workers' wages are cut as a result of the reforms. On other occasions, because of glasnost, workers have felt emboldened to strike over working conditions. Here is a chronology of this year's events.

H The Independent, 24 November, 1988.

I The Independent, 24 November, 1988.

Men who ruled Russia

The problem with the history of Russia in the twentieth century is that it is changing all the time. The changes under Gorbachev have been the most dramatic for a long time. The Bolshevik Revolution did not change everything in Russia suddenly. There was still a secret police and censorship of the press. Life in the countryside was in many ways similar to the way it had been for centuries.

Some of the changes suggested by Gorbachev have been even greater than those brought about by the Revolution. The pictures on these pages give an idea of some of these changes. What other changes have been brought about in Russia since 1988? The history of Russia is a story of continuity and change. These ideas are explored in this revision section.

Sources **A** to **F** show five men who have ruled Russia in the twentieth century. Look back in the book, then make a list of who they were and when they ruled Russia. Remember to put your list in chronological order (earliest at the top, most recent at the bottom).

A

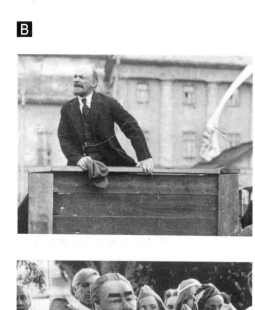

B

C

D

F

E

Romanov to Lenin

Sometimes things change quickly in history – and at other times things seem to stay the same. How much change was there in Russia between 1900 and 1923? What things stayed the same? Copy and complete the chart. Look back in the book to find the missing answers. At the bottom of the chart try to write sentences to sum up your answer or pull your ideas together. Try and explain how big you think the changes were.

Tsar Nicholas' Time (1900)

1 Turn back to page 4.
2 The country was an autocracy. This meant that it was ruled by one man, the Tsar. He had complete power over everything. The people had no power, no vote, no political parties. This had been the situation for centuries.
3 See page 9.

4 Strikes and trade unions were banned, but there were bitter strikes in the new factories in the big cities.
5 See pages 10–11.

6 A few noblemen, landowners and factory owners were fantastically rich, whilst almost all of the rest of the population were very poor. Russia was a very unequal society.
7 The economy was weak and famines broke out from time to time. Land was not used efficiently and there was a shortage of machinery. People often queued for goods.
8 See page 5.

9 See pages 8–11.

10 The ruler of Russia had much in common with the rulers of western Europe. The Tsar was related to many of the European monarchs. Some of their governments were based on a similar set of ideas to those of the Tsar's government. They too were interested in keeping up the power of the monarchy and the church, and making sure that the people didn't have full, democratic power.

Lenin's Time (1923)

1 The country was called the Soviet Union.
2 See page 31.

3 Much of the land had been taken over by the peasants. The state had tried to abolish private property.
4 See page 34.

5 There were factories in only a few big cities. They were owned by the state and, in theory, run by the workers. Production figures for heavy industries like oil, coal, iron and steel were low. There was no consumer goods industry.
6 See page 34.

7 See page 35.

8 Opposition was crushed by the secret police system taken over from the Tsars. Its name was changed to the *Cheka*. Opposition political parties were crushed, and controls were placed on people's freedom of speech. Some of them were sent to prison camps in far away places like Siberia.
9 The country was becoming more technologically advanced but it had been torn apart by World War, Revolutions and Civil War. Technology lagged far behind that of the capitalist West. Much of the peasantry was still uneducated but literacy rates were improving, particularly in the cities. Women were given more equality under the law and were beginning to take up jobs once only done by men.

10 See page 33.

Lenin to Stalin

Sometimes things change quickly in history – and at other times things seem to stay the same. How much change was there in Russia between 1923 and 1939? What things stayed the same? Copy and complete the chart. Look back in the book to find the missing answers. At the bottom of the chart try to write sentences to sum up your answer or pull your ideas together. Try and explain how big you think the changes were.

Lenin's Time (1923)

1 The country was called the Soviet Union.
2 See page 31.

3 Much of the land had been taken over by the peasants. The state had tried to abolish private property.
4 See page 34.

5 There were factories in only a few big cities. They were owned by the state and, in theory, run by the workers. Production figures for heavy industries like oil, coal, iron and steel were low. There was no consumer goods industry.
6 See page 34.

7 See page 35.
8 Opposition was crushed by the secret police system taken over from the Tsars. Its name was changed to the *Cheka*. Opposition political parties were crushed, and controls were placed on people's freedom of speech. Some of them were sent to prison camps in far away places like Siberia.
9 The country was becoming more technologically advanced but it had been torn apart by World War, Revolutions and Civil War. Technology lagged far behind that of the capitalist West. Much of the peasantry was still uneducated but literacy rates were improving, particularly in the cities. Women were given more equality under the law and were beginning to take up jobs once only done by men.
10 See page 33.

Stalin's Time (1939)

1 See page 39.
2 According to the Constitution the people elected the government and had a say in the running of local and national affairs. However there was only one political party, and Stalin gathered huge amounts of power in his own hands. He chose loyal people for important jobs and ruled as a dictator. He was every bit as powerful as the Tsars.
3 See pages 39–40.

4 The use of 'official' government trade unions made it easier for Stalin to control the workers. Strikes were effectively banned.
5 See page 44.

6 The Soviet Union was a more equal society in the sense that the richest nobles, factory owners and churchmen no longer controlled so much of the wealth and power. However there were complaints that a few Communist Party officials were rich, powerful and had expensive houses in the country-side, whilst most of the people struggled.
7 See page 42.
8 Opposition was crushed by a secret police system taken over from Lenin and renamed the NKVD. Spies and informers added to the atmosphere of fear. Freedom of speech and movement were limited. Purges got rid of countless people in the army, civil service and, indeed, in almost every walk of life. Some died in Show Trials. Others just disappeared.
9 There was a big education and technology drive. Stalin ordered his people to catch up the gap of 50–100 years in just 10. Schools, colleges and universities were opened all over the Soviet Union. A tractor industry was created out of almost nothing and new industrial cities sprang up.
10 See page 55.

Events inside Russia

Sources **A** to **E** show important events in Russia this century.

Look back in the book, then make a list of what those events were and when they took place. Remember to put your list in chronological order (earliest at the top, most recent at the bottom).

It will help you to look back at pages 12, 27, 41, 58 and 84.

Stalin to Gorbachev

Sometimes things change quickly in history – and at other times things seem to stay the same. How much chang was there in Russia between 1939 and 1988? What things stayed the same? Copy and complete the chart. Look back in the book to find the missing answers. At the bottom of the chart try to write sentences to sum up your answer or pull your ideas together. Try and explain how big you think the changes were.

Stalin's Time (1939)

1 See page 39.
2 According to the Constitution the people elected the government and had a say in the running of local and national affairs. However there was only only political party, and Stalin gathered great power in his own hands. He chose loyal people for important jobs and ruled as a dictator. He was every bit as powerful as the Tsars.
3 See pages 39–40.

4 The use of 'official' government trade unions made it easier for Stalin to control the workers. Strikes were effectively banned.
5 See page 44.

6 The Soviet Union was a more equal society in the sense that the richest nobles, factory owners and churchmen no longer controlled so much of the wealth and power. However there were complaints that a few Communist Party officials were rich, powerful and had expensive houses in the countryside, whilst most of the people struggled.
7 See page 42.

8 Opposition was crushed by a secret police system taken over from Lenin and renamed the N.K.V.D. Spies and informers added to the atmosphere of fear. Freedom of speech and movement were limited. Purges got rid of countless people in the army, civil service and indeed in almost every walk of life. Some died in Show Trials. Others just disappeared.

9 There was a big education and technology drive. Stalin ordered his people to catch up the gap of 50–100 years in just 10. Schools, colleges and universities were opened all over the Soviet Union. A tractor industry was created and new industrial cities sprang up.
10 See page 55.

Gorbachev's Time (1988)

1 The country was called the Soviet Union.
2 See page 87.

3 Most of the land remained collectivised. However the new, 'glasnost' and 'perestroika' led to a more flexible approach to the economy. Private businesses appeared and more use of private plots of land.
4 See page 87.

5 Big state-controlled factories remained, but there was an attempt to set up small, efficient businesses, borrowing ideas tried successfully in the capitalist West. There were still loud complaints about delays and poor quality, but as the Soviet Union became opened up to new ideas and influences there was a new attempt to improve consumer goods.
6 See page 87.

7 The queues for goods in the shops remained an everyday part of life.
8 See pages 84–85.

9 See pages 84–85.
10 General Secretary Gorbachev still stood for a set of ideas which were vastly different from those of the rival superpower leader, President Reagan of the USA. However this did not stop the two men from holding a series of 'summit' meetings and reaching an agreement to start the reduction of certain types of nuclear weapons. There was room for 'peaceful co-existence' between East and West, and Reagan was prepared to admit that the Soviet Union was no longer the 'evil empire' he had previously described.

Russia and the World

Check your Chronology: 2: Russia and the World

Sources **A** to **E** show five international events in which Russia has been involved this century. Look back through this book and then make a list of what these events were and when they took place. Remember to put your list in chronological order (earliest at the top, most recent at the bottom). It will help if you look at pages 22, 54, 59, 67, 74, and 76.

A

B

C

D

WONDER HOW LONG THE HONEYMOON WILL LAST?

E

93

Glossary

AUTOCRAT A person who rules a country with total power.

BLITZKRIEG German word for 'lightning war' – a war based on fast moving planes and tanks.

BOLSHEVIK Supporter of Lenin before the Revolution. Afterwards the Bolsheviks dropped this name and called themselves Communists.

BOURGEOISIE The middle classes, who sometimes owned factories and businesses.

CHEKA Lenin's secret police, set up in 1917.

COLD WAR A war of nerves and words between the USA and its allies and the USSR and its allies.

COMECON Council of Mutual Economic Aid, set up by Stalin in 1949 to coordinate the development of Eastern European economies.

COMINFORM The Communist Information Bureau, set up in 1947 to organise Communist parties in Europe.

COMINTERN An international organisation set up in 1919 to encourage Communist Revolution throughout the world. Stalin dissolved it in 1943 as a sign of friendship towards his wartime capitalist allies.

COMMISSAR A minister or commissioner.

COMMUNE An organisation in which things are held in common or shared out.

COMMUNISM All land, factories and wealth are shared out in this final stage of history.

COSSACKS Cavalry troops who originally came from southern Russia.

DETENTE The relaxing of tension between USA and the USSR.

DICTATOR A leader who rules with complete power.

DISSIDENT A person who criticises a government, sometimes in a country in which free speech is either limited or banned.

DYNASTY A family of monarchs or rulers who pass power down from one generation to the next.

FIVE YEAR PLAN A set of targets for improvement in the Soviet economy.

GLASNOST The name given to Gorbachev's policy of openness.

G.P.U. State Political Administration or Secret Police, set up in 1922.

GULAG Labour Camp.

KOLKHOZ Collective farm.

KULAK Richer peasant who employed other peasants.

LENINGRAD The city of Petrograd or St Petersburg was renamed Leningrad in 1922 after the dead leader of the Revolution.

MENSHEVIK 'Minority' Communist Party members who split from Lenin at the Communist Party Conference of 1903.

N.E.P. New Economic Policy carried out by Lenin.

O.G.P.U. Unified State Political Administration – or Secret Police, set up in 1924 and reorganised in 1934 as the NKVD. Later it was renamed the KGB.

OKHRANA The Tsar's Secret Police.

POLITBURO The Supreme Committee which leads the Communist Party.

PROLETARIAT The working class.

RED GUARDS Armed Bolshevik supporters.

ST PETERSBURG Russian city built by Tsar Peter the Great in the 17th century. It was given the Russian translation Petrograd (Peter's town) in the First World War because St. Petersburg sounded too German. See Leningrad.

SOCIALISM The stage in which the industries, factories, land etc. are run by the State for the people.

SOVIET Council of soldiers, workers and peasants.

SOVIET UNION The Union of Soviet Socialist Republics (the USSR) was the name given by Lenin's government to Russia.

Acknowledgements

The author and Publisher are grateful to the following for permission to reproduce text extracts, photographs and other illustrative material used in this book:

The Hulton Picture Company 6, 7, 12, 20, 38, 88; David King Collection 5, 8, 9, 11, 14, 15, 18, 19, 22, 23, 30, 32, 34, 36, 41, 45, 48, 52, 53, 56, 62, 63 (C, D), 69 (C), 88, 91, 93; Mansell Collection 10, 25, 50, 99; Novosti Press Agency 16, 27, 39, 40, 41, 43, 44, 91; The Daily Mail 28; National Film Archive 47; Popperfoto 51, 64; Punch 54, 66, 69, 93; St Louis Post-Dispatch 57; School of Slavonic and East European Studies Library 63 (B), 67, 93; Edimedia 70; New Statesman 74, 93; Magnum Photos Ltd 77; Tass News Agency 80, 84, 85, 91; The Independent 86, 86; The Guardian 86, 87; Times Newspapers 86, 87; The Daily Telegraph 87.

Index

Afghanistan   81, 84
agricultural production   33, 37, 41, 42, 68, 78, 84
Alexandra (see Tsarina)
Alexander III   18
Alexis   6, 21
Andropov, Yuri   80
arms race   68, 82–84, 84, 87
atom bomb   64, 68, 82

Berlin Wall   73
Bloody Sunday 1905   12–13, 14, 15, 17, 19, 91
Bolsheviks   17, 18, 19, 20, 25, 26, 27, 28, 29, 32, 33, 34, 46, 94
Brest-Litovsk Treaty   27, 29, 30
Brezhnev, Leonid   76, 80–81, 88

censorship   26, 85
Cheka (secret police)   29, 89, 94
Chernenko, Konstantin   80
church   5, 30, 81
Churchill, Winston   60, 64, 65
Civil War   30, 31–33, 35, 42, 53, 59, 70, 89
Cold War   64–65, 66, 68, 70, 71, 72, 73, 94
collectivisation   37, 38, 41, 46, 48, 68, 75, 81, 84
Comecon   68, 94
communism   4, 16, 18, 33, 36, 64, 65, 75, 94
Communist International   53
Communist Manifesto   16
Communist Party of the Soviet Union (CPSU)   29, 31, 35, 39, 41, 46, 51, 73, 78, 90
communists   4, 31, 37, 55
Constituent Assembly   28, 29
country life   8–9, 37–41, 44, 60
Cuba   82, 83
Czechoslovakia   53, 59, 61, 71, 75–77, 93

Das Kapital   16
Deniken, General   31
detente   80, 94
Domino theory   64, 65
Dubcek, Alexander   75–77
Dulles, John Foster   73, 82
Duma   5, 6, 15, 22, 23, 25

Eastern Europe   56, 59, 60, 61, 64, 66, 68, 70, 72, 75–77
economic problems   10, 33
education   41, 43, 50, 89, 90, 92
Eisenhower, Dwight   72, 73

famine   33, 42, 89
fascism   53
Five Year Plans   37, 38, 42, 68, 78, 94
foreign policy   53–54, 57, 59, 64–65, 73–74, 93

Gapon, Father   12–13
Germany   18, 20, 21, 26, 29, 46, 53, 55, 56, 57–58, 59, 60, 61, 63, 64, 65, 66, 70, 72, 80
Glasnost   70, 84–85, 87, 92, 94
Gorbachev, Mikhail   70, 81, 84–85, 88, 92

GOSPLAN   42
GPU (secret police)   94
Great Patriotic War (see World War II)

H-bomb   68, 73, 82
Hitler, Adolf   47, 53, 55, 57, 63, 93
Hungary   55, 59, 61, 66, 67, 73, 75–77

industrialisation   42–43, 45, 46, 75, 81, 89
industrial production   10, 32, 33, 37, 38, 42, 68, 70, 78, 79, 89
Iron Curtain   65, 66

Kamenev, Lev   36, 46, 47
Kerensky, Alexander   25, 26, 27, 30
KGB (secret police)   94
Khruschev, Nikita   69, 70, 73, 74, 75, 78–79, 80, 82, 88
Kirov, Sergei   46
Kolchak, General   26, 31
Komosomol   80
Korean War   82
Kornilov, General   26, 27, 31
Kulaks   19, 39, 40, 41, 44, 91, 94

labour camps   44, 46, 47, 52, 86, 89, 94
League of Nations   53
Lenin   18, 19, 20, 25, 26, 27, 28–30, 31, 32, 34–35, 37, 50, 51, 52, 53, 68, 78, 84, 88, 89, 90
Leningrad   55, 94

Macmillan, Harold   73, 74
Magnitogorsk   42, 43, 44
Marshall Plan   66–67, 68, 93
Marx, Karl   16, 18, 19
Mensheviks   17, 18, 19, 28, 29, 31, 94
Moscow   30, 31, 51, 52, 84

NATO   67, 71, 72, 73
Nazi-Soviet Pact   53, 54, 55, 56, 80
New Economic Policy (NEP)   33, 36, 37, 42, 94
Nicholas II (see Tsar)
NKVD (secret police)   90, 92
nuclear threat   73, 82, 92

OGPU (secret police)   94
Okhrana (secret police)   5, 20, 89, 94
Operation Barbarossa   55–56, 59, 70, 72

Petrograd   18, 19, 20, 22, 23, 25, 26, 30, 31, 94
Perestroika   84–85, 92
Permanent Revolution   36
Poland   32, 40, 53, 61, 64, 77, 80, 81
Politburo   36, 46, 94
Port Arthur   4, 12
Potsdam Agreement   64–65
proletariat   29
propaganda   38, 41, 50–51, 62–63
Provisional Government   23, 25–27, 28, 29, 30
Purges   46–49, 90, 92

Rapallo, Treaty of   53
Rasputin, Gregory   17, 21, 22, 23
Reagan, Ronald   83, 84, 87, 92
Red Army   31, 32, 33, 46, 58, 60, 63, 66, 70, 75, 77, 80, 81
'Reds'   31, 32
Revolution, 1905   17, 18, 19
Revolution, 1917   18, 20, 21–23, 24, 25, 27, 28, 29, 37, 51, 88, 91
Riga, Treaty of   32
Roosevelt, F.D.   60
Russian Empire   4, 5, 15, 20, 59
Russo–Japanese War   12

St Petersburg   4, 9, 11, 12, 14, 15, 17, 22, 94
SALT (Strategic Arms Limitation Talks)   83
SDI (Strategic Defence Initiative)   82, 83
SEATO   71, 72, 73
secret police   5, 18, 19, 20, 29, 75, 89, 90, 92, 94
show trials   46
Social Democratic Party   17
'Socialism in one country'   36, 37, 43, 53
Social Revolutionary Party   17, 28
Solidarity   77, 80–81
Solzhenitsyn, Alexander   47, 51
Soviets   15, 25, 26, 28, 94
Soviet Union   29, 34, 89, 90, 94 and passim
Spanish Civil War   53
Sputnik   73, 82
Stakhanovites   43
Stalin, Joseph   18, 20, 34, 35, 36, 37, 38, 40, 42–43, 46–47, 48–49, 50–51, 53, 57, 58, 60–61, 64, 68–69, 70–71, 73, 78, 79, 83, 84, 87, 88

Stalingrad   35, 50, 55, 57–58, 60, 91
START (Strategic Arms Reduction Talks)   83
Stolypin, Peter   17

Tannenberg   21
'thaw'   73–74, 82
town life   10–11, 43, 44, 60
Trotsky, Leon   6, 13, 15, 18, 19, 20, 23, 26, 27, 31, 32, 33, 34, 35, 36, 46, 48, 52
Truman Doctrine   64, 65, 66
Tsar (Nicholas II)   5, 6, 7, 8, 12, 13, 14, 15, 16, 17, 19, 21, 22, 24, 88, 89
Tsarina (Alexandra)   5, 6, 7, 9, 21, 22, 23

U2   73, 74, 93
Ulyanov, Vladimir Ilyich (see Lenin)
United Nations Organisation   60, 61, 91
USSR (Union of Soviet Socialist Republics)   38, 42, 53 and passim

Walesa, Lech   81
War Communism   32, 33, 37
Warsaw Pact   67, 71, 72, 73, 75, 76
'Whites'   31, 32
Winter Palace   21, 27
World War I   7, 21–23, 25, 27, 29, 59, 93
World War II   46, 55–56, 57–58, 62–63, 68
Wrangel, General   31, 32

Yalta   60–61
Yugoslavia   68

Zinoviev, Grigory   34, 36, 46, 47